John R. Turner

LETTERS TO DALTON

Higher Education
and the Degree Salesmen

Word and Image
Montpelier, Vermont
2002

LIBRARY.

Word and Image
45 Liberty Street
Montpelier, Vermont 05602

Library of Congress Cataloging-in-Publication Data

Turner, John R. (John Randolph), 1936-
  Letters to Dalton : higher education and the degree salesmen / John R.
Turner.
     p. cm.
   ISBN 0-9723426-0-5 (pbk.)
   1. Diploma mills—United States. 2. Degrees, Academic—United States.
3. Education, Higher—Aims and objectives—United States. 4. Turner,
John R. (John Randolph), 1936—Correspondence. 5. Oliver, Dalton—
Correspondence. 6. Educators—United States—Correspondence.
I. Title.
   LB2388 .T87 2002
   378.2—dc21
                                        2002151890

Printed by Accura Printing
Barre, Vermont

To the memory of my friend
Daniel C. Noel
who always helped me understand
the importance of genuine education

Table of Contents

*I*F YOU'RE GOING to write about education you ought to try to say what it is. Most writers don't and the reason is clear. When you're using a term as an ideological stalking horse, its meaning is best left vague. No word is more snarled now in distortion and demagoguery. Politicians pontificate about it endlessly and show by their language that they haven't bothered to acquire what they claim to be promoting. If "education" has a meaning in current political discourse, it designates only lackluster training processes aimed at cranking out a ready supply of non-critical corporate employees. When a student has enough "education" to get a good job—by which we mean a living wage traded for two thousand hours a year of repetitive performance—then schooling has served the purpose politicians conceive.

That's not the definition of education I'm concerned with here. The term has a nobler heritage which points to the long effort men and women have made to learn how to live the most intelligent lives it is possible to live. When I was a child, the institutions of higher education were thought to be home to education of that sort. The expansion of the university from an exceptional to the expected path to adult life has tended to dilute that ideal. I don't know how many people still hold it, but I do know that the officials who control the majority of American universities are not among them. They don't think of education as enrichment of life because they scarcely think of education at all. They see themselves as managers of institutions whose success is measured by the level of financial activity they generate. Neither their goals nor their methods distinguish them from other business managers. As it's the business of General Motors to sell cars, it's the business of universities to sell degrees.

Some might say that's as it should be. Universities are businesses and they should be managed as businesses. Only then can they flourish and serve a world which increasingly sees capital development as the essential path to a bright future. Yet, there's an older ideal which sets quality of being above material possession and views the university as a community of scholars, students, writers, artists, and thinkers who come together to ask about human purpose and our relation to the nature of things. And this ideal cannot live tranquilly alongside the business model.

The operative delusion in the university world today is that the community of thinkers exists in an awkward but manageable tension with the business mentality. Though it may be seen as regrettable that economic power brokers have wormed their way into positions of authority, they aren't regarded as serious impediments to the university's ongoing educational mission. Few want to face the falsity of that belief because to do so would be to admit that the university has broken its ancient moorings and is launched on a course of public deception made obsessive by the need to deceive not only the customers but the purveyors themselves.

The letters that make up this book were written to explore that obsession and to explain elements of it in common language—a language many segments of the university have dedicated themselves to expunging. They were addressed to Dalton Oliver of Middlebury, Vermont, a physician and former general in the Air Force, who was for a number of years a member of the Board of Trustees of Norwich University, where I worked from 1984 until the fall of 2001.

Dalton and I have been friends since the mid-1980s. Neither of us has been encouraged by what we've seen of higher education lately nor by what seems to lie in store for it. Consequently, we got in the habit of sending critical thoughts, along with clippings and citations, back and forth to one another. Out of this exchange there came the idea that I would write him several letters spelling out what I've observed in the university world over the past generation. These were to be similar in tone to other letters I might write to a friend, but I knew from the start that if I was going to discuss the variety of subjects that came to mind, they would end up being both more extensive and slightly more formal than friendly letters normally are. They were also pushed in the direction of public discourse by our agreement to share them with a few friends and acquaintances .

There are advantages to this mode of writing. Not being put together for a professional audience, it can adopt a conversational frankness academic writing seldom dares approach. And since, for the reader, it constitutes a kind of eavesdropping, no one need apply it to himself. People can read the letters as they wish and take from them what they will. As I said in a note to Richard Schneider, the president of Norwich, written shortly after I began:

> In my letters to Dalton, which, obviously, are more than just ordinary letters, I'm trying to talk about tendencies, inclinations, priorities, and hidden and unconscious motivations. I'm not charging anyone with anything deliberate. That would be foolish on my part and is no part of my desire. I'm also trying to clarify my own thoughts about the ideals of liberal learning. An institution, being part of a hard-nosed world, cannot give its sole attention to ideals. But, in my position, I can. And since so few do it, there's no harm in taking that stance as a way of helping balance the institutional dialogue.

Actually, institutional dialogue may have been what Dalton thought he was getting himself into when he agreed to receive the letters. But it wasn't long before I saw that anything I might say about Norwich could be said about the generality of colleges and universities spread across America. A peculiarity of the literature of higher education—if there can be said to be such a thing—is that most of it assumes that college students go to places with names like Harvard, Princeton, Stanford, and Yale. Truth is, of course, that only a tiny portion of college students are enrolled in such places. Most people go to colleges that are far more like Norwich than they are like Yale. What counts as a college education for the vast majority of Americans is the experience they, or their children, have at middling places which are never going to have Nobel Prize winners on the faculty.

I've frequently encountered an attitude which says, in effect, that Harvard is for Harvard students and most colleges are for people who are going to make their way as insurance salesmen, and Wal Mart managers, and the owners of new car dealerships. The needs of the two groups are entirely different, and there's no sense trying to give what's called a Harvard education to everyone. I hate that attitude. Not having been to Harvard myself, I don't know what a Harvard education is. But if people are using it to symbolize the finest intellectual experience America offers, then I say that every student who enrolls in college should have the chance for an experience similar to what Harvard provides or—to take Harvard out of the metaphor because it's really not Harvard's responsibility to prescribe excellence to the nation—to have an opportunity for the most searching critical and aesthetic experience he or she is capable of enduring.

If that's not realistic, so what? It's what the students should have, and it's what all colleges should be working to approach.

In any case, these letters are about those middling institutions and what the students are getting who pay astounding amounts of money to attend them. It's my contention that the students are getting gypped. That they're unaware of the swindle should be viewed as partial evidence that it's proceeding. Among the many deceptions now bedeviling American life this one may not be at the very top of the list, but since much life energy is devoted to the mid-range universities, their lack of interest in education signals a social turn towards flaccidity that will, ultimately, affect us all.

Though I was happy to write these letters to Dalton alone, I told him from the beginning that I saw him as a surrogate for a body of readers who aren't often addressed on the problems of university education. The university system is self-absorbed and writes mostly to itself. Yet it's presumed to confer benefits throughout the civic structure, and if that really is its role, responsible citizens need to be aware of where it's tending. Their expectations for the university will differ from those who look to it for livelihood and esteem, and, therefore, they need to be addressed in relation to their concerns and in language that steps aside from the obscurities of normal professional discourse.

Within the university, the conceit flourishes that only university people take serious interest in the problems of learning, cultural transmission, and thought. It's a silly idea, but it's strong enough to shape most writing on education, to flavor it to the taste of professors. By contrast, these letters weren't written with professors in mind. They are for Dalton, and readers like Dalton, who care about the university for what it might contribute to the common well-being. I believe there are a great number of people in America who fit that description, and I think, moreover, that they have more to contribute to society's stance on education than they are usually given credit for.

Though I've spoken of Dalton as representing a group, I've always been aware that there's not much groupy about him. He stands apart for me first of all as being among the tiny number of genuinely admirable people I've known. Anyone introducing him in a formal setting would take note of his distinguished career as a physician and an Air Force officer. But, though both these roles have shaped him to a degree, they don't figure much in my thoughts about him. Dalton comes to my mind, first, as a person who would never stab anybody in the back. I used to think that was a norm for most humans, but having scrambled through a majority of my years, I've come to see how rare it is. He cares too much for himself to advance his standing by shabby means. And that, by the way, is a self-concept I think true education naturally supports.

He counts himself as being a lucky man. In a way that's true. He happened on a few opportunities that were unusual for a young general practitioner with a medical degree from the University of Tennessee, including training stints at Harvard and Oxford. But Dalton's too modest to face the truth that his luck has been mostly his character. I've made no effort to study the details of his career, but I'm pretty sure that he got where he did because people who met him knew they could trust him.

He's a few years older than I am and perhaps for that reason has a slightly different perspective on some aspects of the world than I do. But, the grand thing about my friendship with Dalton is I know it doesn't matter. I can say what I think and be sure that Dalton will respect it as honesty from me even if he doesn't agree with it. I'm probably a little more likely to find harmonies in thinkers like Michel Foucault and other post-modern mavens than Dalton is, but I'm confident that I could always talk to Dalton about Foucault, or about any other abstruse subject, and find an interested listener. That's the mark of an educated man. We're both Southerners, and Dalton thinks that has something to do with why we get on. He may be right about that.

I'm saying all this not to puff Dalton. He doesn't need any puffing from me. I'm saying it so that other readers can know to whom these letters were addressed. Their character comes from Dalton as well as from me. Not that I changed my stance to suit his tastes. But having him in mind as I sorted through what I wanted to say gave me the focus I needed. I recall one of Trollope's statements to the effect that a book needs nothing so much as a reader. If that's true of a book, it's double-true of a letter, for the image in the writer's mind of a specific person reading it makes it into a more substantial thing than if it were simply jotted abstractly to express a thought.

The letters themselves will have to bear the main burden of convincing readers—if they're going to be convinced—that something is seriously awry in American colleges and universities. Every writer runs the risk that his own perspective is so colored by peculiar experiences that what he has to say will be meaningless to others. In this case, the danger suggests itself forcefully in that this book isn't like any other you will read about higher education. It's not based on research nor is it a supplement to any professional dialogue. Its main difference, though, from most writing on higher education is that it's not grounded in the assumption that the institutions of higher education are, in and of themselves, of vital significance. I confess to nostalgic feelings about certain of them. I can cheer as fiercely as any fan for Georgia Tech's football team. But, at bottom, I care about universities primarily as agents of education. Everything else they do can be done better elsewhere. And, perhaps, helping people towards education can too. Yet, I think there's enough in the heritage of the university to give education a foothold from which people who care about it, if they wish, might reintroduce it to the center of the universities' concerns.

I would like to see that happen, and I would be especially pleased if these letters would persuade a few people to look critically and lovingly at the universities to which they feel a tie, and try to discover how they might serve them more intelligently than they have in the recent past.

As I mentioned above, I began this series with the notion that my own university could serve as a model for middle-level institutions throughout the land, and that by writing about it I would be commenting honestly about the whole. As I proceeded I discovered that there was no need to maintain the fiction that I was addressing conditions in a single institution. Consequently, if you read on, you'll see that Norwich appears in the first several letters and then fades out of the discourse.

Except for a few minor changes which involved awkwardnesses too gross to be abided, the letters appear here as they were sent out to Dalton in the U.S. mail.

This first letter was more directly addressed to the problems of my institution than any of the others. I considered revising it for general readers by combing most references to Norwich out of it. But I decided not to because I want readers to see the actual sequence of the letters and, more importantly, because Norwich's problems aren't significantly different from those of most other universities. In any case, as the letters proceed the focus shifts quickly from Norwich to the general situation of higher education. The point of this letter is to suggest that struggle among university fiefdoms is a strong reason why academics are diverted from education itself. It may help readers to know that the Brattleboro Center was an outposted, underfunded unit of Norwich designed to rake in money from the population centers around Hartford, Connecticut, and Springfield, Massachusetts. The Adult Degree Program, or ADP, is one of the multitude of low residency programs for students older than the traditional college age which sprang up in the 1960s and 1970s as the managerial model began to dominate American higher education.

I WAS HAPPY to get your call the other day. Your determination to think through the problems of the university and help it move in a healthy direction is one of many things I admire about you. Our conversation got me to thinking that I ought to put my own perceptions of Norwich's situation on paper, and, since you have an appetite for speculation, to send them to you, while giving a few other people a chance to eavesdrop on our conversation.

Every organization needs to remember that its success depends on having a firm grasp of its principal goal. For universities in Norwich's range there are only two possibilities. Primary attention can be given to education or it can be put to selling degrees. There's a spurious shrewdness at work in higher education nowadays which argues that universities must do both in order to survive. But no institution can do both equally. One goal will come before the other, and the one that's given the first place determines how the other is pursued.

When the two goals are mentioned bluntly, lip service is always paid to education. "Education is, of course," the institution will say, "our first goal." But that kind of statement's not worth a hill of beans. We find out what the real goal is by listening to what people say and watching what they do, by investigating how they spend their time, and by uncovering the subjects of their common deliberations. I have no measuring stick to tell me for sure what Norwich's prime goal is, but a good deal of the talk I've heard lately says that if degree-selling is not now on top, it's creeping in that direction.

Organizations are free to choose their own purposes. There's nothing to say that Norwich can't, if it wishes, operate like a business for the simple reason of doing business. But if that's to be what it's about, it probably ought to come clean and adopt the practices of hard-nosed selling currently fashionable in the marketing world. I can't predict how successful it might be in that mode because I don't care about it. I've been mixed up with trying to educate for so long that I'm not capable of going over to the business side. On the other hand, if we speak of education as the prime goal, then I do have an idea of how the subsidiary goal—the business goal—should follow.

The sense I get from occasionally hearing university officials talk is that they think the educational efforts of the university are in good shape and that what the university now needs is a skillful business strategy to produce increased "revenue streams," which, if they become sufficiently turgid, will solve the university's problems. This is an attitude which, whether consciously or not, puts degree-selling in the first place. Educational practice tags along after it and consequently can never be anything other than a grafting on of conventional thought which produces, by definition, mediocrity. As we know from the history of American business, the selling of mediocrity requires ever-increasing intensity of advertising. Since one product is virtually indistinguishable from most others, the only way to sell it is to push it harder than the competitor does and, often, to imply something that's not perfectly true. One is forced into the strategy of the major aspirin companies. If one were to chart the budgets of the so-called "admissions" offices of Norwich over the past thirty years, the sky-rocketing costs might give a sense of whether, or not, that's the strategy Norwich has been trying to follow.

A version of the business strategy that has been popping up lately and that appears to be particularly lively in my portion of the university—the Adult Degree Program—is the notion that salvation lies in enhanced delivery systems. The belief grows that placing words on paper is becoming impossibly onerous for modern-day folk: it's too slow, too laborious, too hideously old-fashioned. On the other hand, if we'll transmit our thoughts electronically, and package them in units that might be called electronic modules, and commit ourselves to instantaneous response to student impulse, then we'll be up to date, popular, and "viable," as people now say. No matter that we're dealing in the same old droopy thoughts. They'll have a new look, and in selling degrees, the look is all important. There's a certain appeal to this approach. The look is important. But, over the long run, unless it's merely the surface of a sustaining core, it will fade, and then all we can do is hustle yet again for another new look.

As you know, my daughter Emily will be graduating from the University of Virginia in a couple of months. As I look back over Emily's experience with the University, I realize that it made no exaggerated efforts to recruit her class. It accepts only about 20% of out-of-state applicants, and that percentage continues to decline as the numbers of applicants increase. In short, it has no difficulty getting students, and in that respect it is similar to about three percent of the more than three thousand colleges and uni-

versities in the United States. What is it about the three percent that sets
them apart from Norwich?

The answer comes readily. Each of them projects an educational tone
which bespeaks a version of excellence. Sure, they're similar to one another in many ways, and they're similar to less distinguished institutions.
But, along with their similarities, each has a distinct educational personality which proclaims in unmistakable terms that if you come you will be
among people who put education first and you will receive an education
that you can get nowhere else. That's a powerfully attractive message. The
trouble with it is that it can't be credibly advanced solely by PR manipula-
tions; it has to be grounded, to some extent, in the educational reality of
a place.

I've been out of touch with many segments of Norwich so long that I don't
know exactly how such a personality could be developed for the whole of
the university. I just know it has to be created if Norwich is to succeed as an
institution which puts education first. A revitalized personality would require a sense of purpose rising both from the university's past and from
intelligent new actions. And, to bring it into being would take conscious
intent and vigorous internal dialogue.

I am, however, in fairly close touch with one small portion of the university, and so I do know how the right personality for it could be developed.
The ADP has been a decent educational effort for some years now. But it
has been in educational stasis, and I suspect it has reached the limit of
attractiveness that its current educational quality permits. Without an
enhanced educational vitality, it probably can't be made to grow.

To transform it into a program that doesn't have to worry about enroll-
ments would require a clearer view of its potential than it has now. The
ADP has major strengths, but it doesn't fully understand them. Nor does
it understand how some of its persistent bad habits continue to drag
it down.

It's hard for people who haven't taught adults to imagine how hungry they are, when they finally do get themselves into an educational setting, to explain their own being to themselves, to think through the fundamental questions of their lives. It may be that eighteen-to-twenty year old people are less ready for the style of education that enables adults to come into their own. I'm unsure about the younger students since I've been away from teaching them for quite a while, though I think the same principles apply to them as to people of any other age. I do know that trying to deal with the kind of students the ADP attracts by using the style of conventional class-room teaching is a travesty. This, I think, the program does understand (though that understanding may be fading).

What the program doesn't realize as well as it should is what's necessary to help people toward authentic lives. The program has suffered from addiction to propaganda for so long that although it has begun to make halting steps towards ridding itself of the vice, it has a way to go, and it doesn't seem to be generating the energy to push on through. The notion that one can fix people up by plopping the right ideology on their heads persists to some extent (though it's not as strong as it used to be).

Probably the main reason the ADP has missed its potential is that it has always run away from the problem of curriculum. The curriculum as defined collectively by the individual choices of the students is not strong. If one were to collect for a year all the items that appear on the study bibliographies of ADP students and publish them in a big list, the results would be frightening. They would be frightening, in part, for what is included, but they would be even more frightening for what is not. This is the reason you will never see such a list, even though, with the ADP's vaunted new technological propensities, it would be easy to produce. But, no one in authority wants to look at it.

The argument against improving the curriculum has been the program's commitment to independent study. But, there's no reason we couldn't remain just as firmly wedded to independent study as we are now and still lead the students to richer study materials.

Nobody can take charge of his or her own existence by reading how-to books, or by parroting Hallmark-card slogans, or by pasting a fashionable ideology onto oneself. The reason there are complex thoughts available in the human community is that human life is complex. The only way students can escape the automaton existence cheap morality would foist on them (and most of them genuinely do want to escape it) is to get themselves into dialogue with voices that reflect long, hard thought and that have stood the test of time. I am weary of watching people proceed through the program who haven't read a play by Shakespeare, who haven't read a poem of Wordsworth's, who haven't read a novel by Jane Austen, who have never heard of the quadratic equation, and who can't tell the difference between Immanuel Kant and Immanuel Velikovsky. Though it's true that there is no perfect core curriculum, and that we shouldn't be seeking to establish one, it's also true that we should be helping students towards study materials that are complex enough, rich enough, and demanding enough that the students will be encouraged to bring out their own authentic selves by encountering them.

I could go on for a long time about the details of teaching in this mode. But that would be to turn a letter into a book (at the time I wrote this letter I wasn't yet aware that was exactly what I was going to do). The last point I need to address in the letter itself is the mechanism needed for the ADP to move towards realizing its potential. It can't be a top-down process; it has to rise up out of specific faculty work. And the predicament is that the faculty does very little work together. The small group I'm a part of in Brattleboro is a case in point. It's made up of reasonable, energetic, and good-hearted people. The meager common work we have managed, in the inadequate time we have, shows me, beyond doubt, what we could achieve if we had the time and energy to confer about our collective tasks and to call on past experience. If that same group, building on the base it has already constructed, could have several hours each residential weekend to work systematically on the best methods to help students approach their potential, and if the consistency of that work were sufficiently valued to extend it over a couple years, the experience of the students in the group would become so much richer and so much more valuable to them that they would be transformed into invaluable ambassadors to the wider world. Send out students over a number of years who have had that quality of education and who can demonstrate the results of it, and a steady influx of new students will be assured. But that won't happen. The program administration is already involved in contortions designed to address momentary budget issues that will break the group apart by next fall. Any collective wisdom it might have begun to amass will be fragmented and drained away.

There's little staying power in the ADP because there's little staying power in the university. Each panics at the slightest downturn and consequently lives in continuous crisis. I'm reminded of a lesson I was taught years ago when I was working for the federal government and went to a seminar conducted by Roger Hilsman, who was the assistant secretary of state for Far Eastern Affairs. "Gentlemen," he said as we were breaking up, "Keep in mind that this town is inhabited mostly by crisis managers. If they didn't have a crisis to manage they wouldn't have an idea in hell of what to do. So, they make sure they always have one."

Forgive me for droning on so long. People tell me I shouldn't write this sort of stuff. But, talking in this vein to a friend is a way of getting my thoughts straight. And sometimes I have to get them onto paper so they won't stay in my head and drive me crazy. This particular subject draws me because when things go right with my student group, I know they're getting something from the experience they can't get anywhere else, something they not only treasure but find essential. If we could clarify that experience to ourselves and the world, Norwich wouldn't have to worry about enrollees. My saying so won't make any difference, but perhaps there's an idea or two here that you can carry round with you and put into play sometime when it might have a chance to take hold.

The articles mentioned below point to higher education's confusion about its priorities. Although many observers recognize the devalued condition of education in the universities, they can't get at the problem because the focus of their concern remains the university organization rather than the quality of mind it ought to be serving.

I GOT THE packet with your two commentaries and the two op-ed pieces when I got home from a quick trip to Charlottesville to spend some time with Emily. I went down there because she's finishing up her honors thesis on Thomas Hardy and wanted to talk over a few points about a concept of advanced consciousness he treated in several of his novels.

At any rate, I came to the pieces you sent with Hardy's notions of advanced consciousness in mind, and that probably had some effect on how I read them. Emily's main argument at the end of her paper is that Hardy leaves us uncertain about the future of the discriminating and sensitive mind he saw emerging at the end of the 19th century. Was it going to turn out to be thoughtful, considerate, and just, producing a desirable and meaningful society? Or was it going to turn out to be merely crazy, too neurotic to deal with the realities of existence?

Here we are a hundred years later, and we don't yet know the answer. There's some evidence that craziness is winning out. People are eating more pills than they ever ate before, and feeding them to their little kids. The notion that somebody might love somebody else and have that love last more than fourteen months appears ever more remote. Most of those who rant about morality, religion, and development of soul are pursuing only money and

power. In education, the confusion among the people in charge has rock-
eted to levels we didn't even know existed when you and I were young. So,
as always, there's plenty of evidence the world is going to hell.

Still, I don't think it is. These are troublesome phenomena, but I suspect
they're mainly on the surface and that underneath, down in the social unconscious from which new worlds emerge, exciting and wonderful things
are happening. The serious question for any university which puts education first is how to get in touch with those positive forces and help them
emerge with as little pain and misery as possible. Of course, to get in touch
with something you've got to have an inkling of what it is, and that points
to the university's most profound weakness at the moment.

The essay you sent by Teresa Ebert and Mas'ud Zavarzadeh on how so-
called "net education" puts content above all else was very fine. Their point
about distinguishing education from training is the most important perception a university can have. And their statements about how education
takes place are essentially correct, although I think the process can be described more distinctly than they manage in the short space they have (I
want to take a shot at a more adequate description in one of my future
letters to you).

I suspect that those who are engaged in training think that voices which set
education above it are either elitists or snobs, and that they have no conception of the vast amount of training that's necessary to make the world
work. And, they're probably right about some of their critics. But, setting
education above training doesn't require disparagement of the latter. Of
course it's important. If there's one thing I've retained from earning an
engineering degree at Georgia Tech it's a deep respect for the people who
pump clean water to our houses, and make electricity available to us, and
keep the roads repaired, and so on. Doing all that requires an immense
store of knowledge, and it's not knowledge anybody is born with. People
have to be trained to do these things, and it's not simply a matter of rote
training, either. They have to learn how to improvise, and think through
problems, and to devise specific solutions.

Everyone who lies down at night in a warm, clean house owes a debt to the training and systems that make that possible.

Even so, all the finely functioning physical systems the human mind can devise won't teach us how to be with ourselves and other people. The quality of being (or Being, as it's sometimes presented in philosophical treatises) is the subject of education. Since existence, in its fundamental nature, is primary and comes before particular modes of existence, and particular professional, national, and ethnic identities, then education should hold the first place—before training. And the university that doesn't put it there is claiming to be something it's not. That's not to say that universities can't engage in training. But they can't put training first.

The article about the soul of a new university from the *New York Times* by Arthur Levine makes several good points. But, it's insufficiently informed by an understanding of the difference between training and education, which is, I guess, what you would expect from the president of a teachers college, even the Teachers College. The reason is that Levine is concentrated on how to insure institutional health rather than on how to pursue education. He wants the universities of the future to "get with it," to face the technological changes that are coming, to downgrade the importance of bricks and mortar, to plunge body and soul into the internet. All that's okay, I suppose. But if it's done with no understanding of why, of what educational goals are being pursued, then all it's really about is selling degrees, which is the temptation currently plucking mightily at the university's soul.

I guess it would be a great thing to be the premier degree salesman of the world. But, between you and me, I can't figure why anybody should give a damn.

I loved your commentary about endowments and boards of trustees. It reminded me that last November 16th, I jotted this entry in my journal: "Boards of trustees are generally composed of people who care too little for knowledge because they care too much for money." That's been true of every board I've known, but it was true of the Norwich Board, when I was

familiar with it, to an insane degree. Rumor has it that the board of trustees now is considerably less Neanderthal than the board was in the middle
80s, that the influence of the gunpowder and horse shit crowd has been
diminished. I hope that's true but, of course, I have no way of knowing.
Many board members are incapable of caring about education because they're
innocent of it themselves. All they can think to do is to put money in the
place of education, so that the size of the endowment—rather than the
habits of mind of the graduates—becomes for them the measure of the
university. It's hard to have conversation with people in that frame of mind
because when you propose spending money to enhance education you are,
from their point of view, wanting to spend it on nothing, wanting, in effect,
to throw it away. They do, though, have this in their favor. They're aware
that the faculty can't distinguish between spending money for education
and spending money to make themselves more comfortable. Consequently,
they're suspicious that costly reform measures are designed to benefit the
faculty and do nothing else. They're right to be suspicious.

What's needed is the very thing the university at the moment can't sustain:
an ongoing conversation about the purposes of education which could, if it
were ably led, eventuate in activities we could be reasonably sure were worth
the resources they required. The decision to spend money on education is
worth little if we don't know how to spend it. I recall one day I was sitting
in the first row in the chapel at Vermont College beside Russ Todd (president of Norwich in the 1980s) at a ceremony of some sort when he leaned
over and whispered, "Boy! Wouldn't it be great if we had the money to do
all the things here at Vermont College we'd like to do?" And, I responded,
"Yeah, it would help us get to hell even faster than we're going already." It
may have been comments like that which caused Russ to suspect that I
might not, really, be on the team. But I was simply trying to make the same
point to him that I had tried to make many times before: we need to understand our purposes better before we can know how to spend our money
wisely. That's just as true today as it was then. Though, since his presidency, the university has improved in civility, it has not improved in knowing its own mind. In fact, I think Russ, for all his shortcomings, was more

supportive of fundamental inquiries of that kind than the current administration has been.

It would be a fine thing if, as you propose, we could start up a university center in Manchester or some other intelligently selected place. But the first thing we would need to build into the core of it would be an ongoing commitment to inquire into educational purpose. Unless it were animated by a spark of that kind, it could degenerate into one more inadequately furnished and staffed outpost, descending into disgruntlement. Even so, new beginnings offer new opportunities. It probably would be easier to bring fresh thinking to a new center than to persuade established parts of the university to relinquish bad habits. And good practices exhibited in the new place could, over time, return to refresh the old.

I'm looking forward to your getting back here, so we can have lunch and thrash over all these things.

As I approached the third letter I began to realize I had got myself into something more complicated than I had intended. Like some others in the university community, I had a feeling for what education is. But I was largely inarticulate when it came to speaking of it. I shared the delusion that one should be able to define education during cocktail party chatter, in two-minute snippets, and I was reluctant to face the inanity of that thought. If I learned anything from struggling to write these letters to Dalton, it's that complex entities have complex definitions and that a concept as sweeping as education requires ongoing thinking. One is never done with it.

*T*ODAY BEING MY first birthday of the new millennium, perhaps it's appropriate that I give attention to something moderately fundamental. So, I'm going to begin trying to describe the core experience of education. It is reluctance to make efforts of this sort that keeps common talk of education swirling in circles, always chasing its tail so to speak. It's persistently circular because it fails the challenge of definition. I probably can't succeed completely, but I think I can hint at a few features of the goal we should be pursuing.

In loose talk there are hundreds of ways to speak of education. Almost any kind of activity that conveys information from one person to another can be called educative. And that's all right for loose talk, which we all engage in from time to time. But when we get down to speaking of what we're trying to accomplish in a university, loose talk will no longer serve .

If a university is going to exist for the purpose of education rather than for selling degrees, at least a goodly portion of its members need to understand what essential experience it's trying to promote. Right now, at most universities, there hasn't been enough conversation on this subject to insure that a quorum has an inkling of what's being attempted. That's why the university's efforts for achieving institutional security start from a place of confusion.

Possession of a sense of the core educational duty is what separates the sheep from the goats in higher education. The two hundred and fifty, or so, institutions which know at least a little of what education is about are clearly different in tone and mission from the other three thousand which stumble along, concerned primarily with paying the bills and staying in business just for the sake of the business. I don't want to overpraise the distinctive institutions. They too are undermined by a flat and generally pedantic view of education. But at least they have one of some sort.

The article you sent from the Tucson *Citizen* by Teresa Ebert and Mas'ud Zavarzadeh makes the point that the thrust towards so-called "net" education is designed to serve the lower classes and keep them in their traditional position. It's a worthwhile argument and reminds us that, as much as we like to pretend that class plays no part in higher education, it is, in truth, the ruling consideration. I'm reminded that once at a Parents' Day reception a father asked me to define the liberal arts, and I told him they are the studies the privileged class has taught to its children so they can remain on the top of the heap.

Education, among other things, is the activity of persons who believe that their own lives have intrinsic meaning, whereas training is the activity of people who are being designed as tools. There's nothing wrong with the latter. We're all tools for other people in some respects. But, if that's all we are, if education plays no part in our life's purpose, then we surrender much of our humanity. If you listen to the common discourse about higher education, if you, for example, read *The Chronicle of Higher Education* regularly, you get the sense that many people believe that's exactly what we're supposed to do.

It's a peculiar attitude: this notion of human being as tool, and tool alone. It doesn't fit with the reality of who we are. Try as one will to be a tool every minute of every day, or, as most people put it, "to keep busy," a goodly portion of our time is spent simply being with ourselves. It's the quality of what happens when people are simply being that's the core subject of education.

One of the common tales of our time is the distress of active men when they are forced to retire before they want to. One hears them pleading, over and over, with a note of despair in their voices, "I have to have something to do." They're desperate to avoid having to exist with themselves, because they're unable to think of themselves as creatures of intrinsic value. They have been trained to be tools; they have not been educated to be persons. And when they confront the possibility of non-tooldom, they're terrified. Anything to keep busy! Anything to escape having to face their own humanity!

In Jane Austen's novel *Emma*, the title character walks out on the stoop of a shop in the little village of Highgate and looks up and down the street. Nothing out of the ordinary is going on, and, then, in the background, we hear the author's voice telling us that's okay: "A mind lively and at ease can do with seeing nothing, and can see nothing that will not answer." This simple passage goes a long way towards telling me what the core task of education is: we are responsible for helping bring forth minds lively and at ease.

Probably the chief difficulty in higher education now is that the people who are charged with promoting and protecting the core task have lost the ability to speak of it effectively. Professors tend to use such stale language when they talk about education few can stand to listen to them. Truth is, they can scarcely stand to listen to themselves. When attempting to lay out what liberal education is for, they drop into hackneyed phrases like "the whole person," or "human completeness," or "humane values," or "the cultivated mind," and so forth. There's no way to make people believe in such notions because nobody can figure out what they mean. That's doubtless because they don't mean very much. Rather, phrases of that kind constitute the rhetoric of a coddled, mandarin class which expects people to genuflect just because it assumes a sanctified tone.

I run the risk myself. But, at least, I'm aware of it. That's why I'm always reminding my students that it's the quality of existence in their own heads and hearts that measures the quality of their education. They don't have to buy into anybody else's rhetoric. They don't have to care whether they're cultured, or not. They don't have to be anybody else's version of a whole person. What they do have to do is get up everyday and live with themselves. They have to face the issue of whether who they are, in their own being, is right, is enough, is as it ought to be.

Don't think I'm going ga-ga on you, or New Age, or mystical, or spiritual, or moony. I don't get my students to chant mantras, or walk through mazes, or sniff anything. What I do try to help them with is developing habits of mind that permit them to interact with the world intensely. Suppose a person who had never heard of the American Civil War went to Gettysburg. All he would see is a moderately pleasant little Pennsylvania town with some monuments in fields off to the side. But, if he knew what had happened there on the 1st, 2nd, and 3rd of July in 1863, and if he had entered imaginatively into those events and tried to fathom how they had affected the people who participated in them, then it would no longer be a common town; it would be a place of terrible magic. And his heart and his soul would come alive. The difference in the two experiences defines what I mean by education. In one case the experience is infused by education; in the other, it is not. An educated person is one who interacts habitually with the world in the way a fervid student of the Civil War interacts with Gettysburg.

I can easily imagine that a hard-nosed theorist of institutional behavior might say to me that it's well to talk up the good of intense interaction, but that experiences of that sort are dependent on the orientation a student brings to his or her studies, and that there's not much a teacher can do to affect it. This is the old "you can lead a horse to water but you can't make him drink" argument. I've heard lots of people use it in a variety of ways. But, I've never heard it used for any other reason than to excuse bad teaching. It's simply not true that you can't help students bring their minds alive. It can be done if one wants to put in the effort to do it. And that's what an institution that puts education first will do.

The first step in helping students come alive is to recognize it as our primary goal. It comes before pouring information down their gullets; it comes before indoctrinating them with messages; it comes before impressing them with what great scholars we are; it comes before insisting that they know how to put their footnotes in the proper form. When we have minds alive, and vital, and questioning, and critical then all these other things come in due turn and take on their proper importance. But when we have minds that are dull, and propagandized, and formulaic, and plodding, it doesn't matter how correct our footnotes are, because any note that might be used will be in support of things better left unsaid.

If an institution seeks to awaken its students it must itself be alive. You've understood this thoroughly, and that's why you pushed to establish the lecture series that now bears your name. But what you understand, others do not. There seems to be a notion that if we collect a batch of people with elegant credentials in the vicinity of one another, then thought will take place, and this thought will then slosh over onto the students. It's as simple as that: the talking-head-in-the-room theory of education. Unfortunately, there is scarcely a more flawed or pathetic idea. Without a vital internal dialogue, the mind of the university can be, and usually will be, just as lethargic as a freshman sleeping in the back row of his chemistry class.

I realize that saying we ought to bring the minds of our students alive by having living minds ourselves doesn't explain how to do it. That, I have to leave for subsequent missives. Here I've wanted to make only one simple point: a university education worthy of the name has to be dedicated primarily to awakening the minds of students in the interest of intense existence, in the interest of intense interaction with the world. That definition of education must be established if I'm to have a chance to make sense in later letters.

It's not, after all, a radical concept. Trace the history of thought back as far as we can go and you find people saying pretty much the same thing. Pindar, in the 5th Century B.C. was fond of advising: "Become what you are," which is simply another way of telling us to bring out the intensity of our own being. Martin Heidegger in the 20th century took Pindar as one of his models. Why can't we learn from these people?

I have some thoughts about that too, which I'll try to bring out, gingerly, as we go along. I say "gingerly" because the reason we don't do as we ought isn't complimentary to some of us. My purpose is not to insult anybody, but, on the other hand, I'm not in the mood to be muffled either. As Dick Hathaway said to me today on the phone: "My God, Turner: we're at an age when there's no reason to hold back any more." I guess I'll take him as my guide.

I promised myself that I would keep these letters in the neighborhood of two thousand words, and we're about at the limit. So, I'll stop for tonight. A guy on his birthday needs to leave a minute or two to eat a slice of cake.

As I worked my way into the fourth letter I started to have a vague sense of the scope I needed to realize my intentions. I knew that this was a subject one could write on forever and, consequently, that limits of some kind had to be imposed. I wasn't yet sure of all the topics I wanted to take up, but as I asked myself what might constitute a reasonable length for the project, a total of thirty-six letters suggested itself, and from then on I proceeded with that number in mind.

Y OU MAY HAVE noticed that Saul Bellow is out with a new novel, *Ravelstein*, based on the life of Allan Bloom, who made a stir thirteen years ago with his book *The Closing of the American Mind.* The response to Bloom's book was more interesting than the book itself. There were howls of indignation from the liberal faculty members of America, because Bloom, in effect, charged them with intellectual treason. I recall that at the time I thought the reaction was overdone. There were features of *The Closing of the American Mind* I didn't agree with, and even a few parts that were a little goofy. But, at the same time, it made some points that were worth consideration.

Here's what Bellow, in the first chapter of the novel, has to say about the effect of the reception overall:

> Well, his friends, colleagues, pupils, and admirers no longer had to ante up in support of his luxurious habits. Thank God, he could now do without the elaborate trades among his academic pals in Jensen silver, or Spode or Quimper. All of that was a thing of the past. He was now very rich. He had gone public with his ideas. He

had written a book—difficult but popular—a spirited, intelligent, warlike book, and it had sold and was still selling in both hemispheres and on both sides of the equator. The thing had been done quickly but in real earnest: no cheap concessions, no popularizing, no mental monkey business, no apologetics, no patrician airs. He had every right to look as he looked now, while the waiter set up our breakfast. His intellect had made a millionaire of him. It's no small matter to become rich and famous by saying exactly what you think—to say it in your own words, without compromise.

I have little hope that these letters to you can rival Bloom's work in either courage or originality. And of one thing we can be sure: nobody's going to make millions from them. I do hope though that I can write them with no mental monkey business, no apologetics, and no patrician airs. If I'm successful then it's probably inevitable that I'll be mildly irritating to some. I regret that. I don't want to irritate anybody just for the sake of irritation. Yet when it comes to a choice between being agreeable and telling the truth as one can best tell it, there's not much question about what to do.

I'm thinking of these things because last week I was chided, in a small way, for suggesting that Norwich might be in the business of selling degrees. About this, there is no question. Of course it's in the business of selling degrees. All universities are in the business of selling degrees. If they weren't, they couldn't stay in operation. The issue is not whether a university is selling degrees. The issue is what it is selling degrees for. Is it selling degrees in order to do education? Or does it do some semblance of education in order to sell degrees? Does education come first, or does the selling come first? Those were the questions I was raising in the first letter in this series.

What my critic was actually objecting to was my failure to observe the euphemisms of higher education. Spokespersons for universities don't speak of selling degrees, because they want to turn the public's attention away from that aspect of the business. They want to pretend that universities and colleges are concentrated on the nobler features of life. They want to suggest that within the university idealism is so strong the vulgar characteristics of life outside have no chance to prevail. They want to act as though back-biting, and vested interest, and intellectual laziness, and cheap taste have no foothold within the sacred halls. The truth, though, is that when we forget that these things are always present, eager to rise up and take over, we almost ensure their triumph. If the price of liberty is eternal vigilance then the price of education is never-flagging critical self-scrutiny.

G. B. Grundy, in his little memoir, *Fifty-five Years at Oxford*, tells the story of a crotchety old don who was in the habit of reminding his colleagues that during the three years the faculty had the students in their charge little more could be achieved than to point them in the direction of adequate knowledge, but, at least, the professors could teach them how to know when someone was talking rot. It wasn't a bad definition for undergraduate education, and it causes me to reflect that in recent years it has become increasingly difficult of realization because the public gush of rot has become so powerful no student can altogether avoid it. For this reason, I'm not in the mood to speak euphemistically—at least not in these letters—so I had best confess, in advance, my inclinations in that respect.

It has seemed to me that careful attention to words is the primary instrument of liberal education. R. G. Collingwood has said that those who use words to mean what they don't in fact mean are poisoning the well of civilization. If that's true then the examination of words comes before anything else in liberal learning. It comes before indoctrinating people into disciplines. It comes before stuffing them with information. It comes even before building their self-esteem, which for those of a psychological persuasion seems to have taken over as the primary function of schooling. The reason words are so important is that students who fail to develop a critical stance towards them can be made to believe anything. In the grip of unexamined language a person will surrender his independence and become a puppet dancing on strings he doesn't know exist.

A slack approach to language has created problems universities scarcely know how to address. For one thing, it has made a shambles of the undergraduate curriculum. The traditional subjects of study were supposed to be founded on careful scrutiny of meaning and tight use of language. But as the curriculum has expanded to include anything anybody might pursue as a vocation, the quality of the language used in some disciplines has become laughable. We now find legions of Ph.D.s who can scarcely write an English sentence because they have been taught by people who care nothing for the quality of English sentences. Language practice in some fields has become notorious for its inanity. An example of how bad things have become is a document titled *The Vermont Framework of Standards and Learning Opportunities* which is supposed to explain to public school teachers in Vermont what they should teach their students. Yet, it's couched in language so flaccid and abstract it can't be used for its designated purpose. The saddest thing about it is that the people who wrote it can't understand what's wrong with it because they, themselves, are so poorly educated they don't know the difference between good and bad words. And, it is they who are supposed to be leading our children to the educational promised land.

You'll recall that in the mid-1980s we had numbers of investigations and reports spawned by the National Commission on Excellence in Education and its little booklet "A Nation at Risk." Andrew Hacker, commenting on some of them in the *New York Review* of February 13, 1986, noted that "the three reports on higher education are most severe on college faculties. All three rate the general run of teachers as mediocre or indolent, with most professors indifferent to larger educational aims." Why this should have been the case when American universities were achieving the most highly credentialed faculties in their history struck some as a mystery. But, there's nothing at all mysterious about it. Most of these credentials were being awarded in fields where people are not taught to read and write, and where candidates can proceed to post-doctoral studies without digesting a single substantial book.

This brings me back to the point with which I started in the first letter. When universities do not put education first, but are more concerned with "advancement" or "achievement," including their own business success, the result is degraded language. Christopher Lasch made this point more forceibly than I can in an article he published in *Harper's Magazine* for September 1990:

> When words are used merely as instruments of publicity and propaganda, they lose their power to persuade. Soon they cease to mean anything at all. People lose the capacity to use language precisely and expressively, or even to distinguish one word from another. The spoken word models itself on the written word instead of the other way around, and ordinary speech begins to sound like the clotted jargon we see in print. Ordinary speech begins to sound like "information"—a disaster from which the English language may never recover.

Why are professors "mediocre" or "indolent"? Because they don't have the language to persuade, and they are not dealing with material that has the language to persuade. They "lose the capacity to use language precisely and expressively" because no one has taught them "to distinguish one word from another."

There always have been dull teachers, and there probably always will be. But a dull teacher can be partially redeemed by fine material. Ann Hulbert in her essay "The Curriculum Commotion," which appeared in *The New Republic* for May 6, 1985, made the argument succinctly:

> Of course great teachers help bring great books to life; but even in the hands of mediocre professors, such books are arguably more instructive than the introductory schemes those professors are likely to carve out of their own specialties.

When those specialties are nothing but great glops of special pleading, designed only to help people climb up ladders, impress superiors, make money, and achieve success, and when the mandarins of those specialties have never given a second thought to the sanctity of the word, then the poor student is really in the soup and may as well doze while waiting to take the exam and get the credit, which is all he's paying his money for anyway.

I spoke earlier of my frustration over the inability of my program, the ADP, to move closer to its potential. It's a frustration made all the more poignant by the ADP's having sought, in some ways, to base its teaching on the importance of careful language. We could do more than we are doing if we could keep our eyes steadily on that foundation stone and, somehow, rescue time from our busy-ness to confer with one another about how to do it effectively and intelligently. The ADP, though, isn't exempt from the pressures of the world around it, and if it doesn't find the means to re-energize itself educationally, it too can be swept away by miseducational currents. It's pretty much in the position Diane Ravitch has attributed to the generality of American undergraduate programs. Writing in *The American Scholar* in the Spring Edition of 1984, she said, "Pedagogical practice follows educational philosophy, and it is obvious that we do not yet have a philosophical commitment to education that is sound enough and strong enough to withstand the erratic dictates of fashion." I have hoped that the ADP (and Norwich to a lesser extent) could commit itself to an educational philosophy based on careful attention to language. Over the long run nothing else would make it as attractive to students, and nothing else could inoculate it as well against cheap and destructive fashion. Hoping, though, is not, in itself, enough.

Here I have got to my two thousand words faster than I meant to. I was going to say something about being educationally serious without stepping over the line into fanaticism. After all, we don't want to drive ourselves nuts. But, I'll leave that for another time.

Thanks for reading.

With this letter I introduced a theme which continued to influence my thought all the way through the rest and which I've since come to designate as "collaboration through seeming conflict." Faculty members chatter endlessly about the philistinism of administrators, but in truth they're pleased with managers who care nothing for education because they divert attention from the faculty's slightly less radical neglect of the subject.

I FINISHED LAST time saying I didn't want to get fanatical about our conversations on education. Fanaticism, to my mind, is never a good thing. On the other hand, I'm reminded of a time when I was a boy and our coach had been working us pretty hard. One of the other guys had seen an article about the dangers of over-training which said that if you pushed yourself too much you could damage your muscles and lose ability. He brought it up to the coach, who eyed him coolly before answering: "I'll tell you what, boy. You ain't close yet."

I'm not worried that anyone I've met is going to strain himself thinking too hard about education.

If there is a sense that we shouldn't be wasting our time deliberating over how to teach and learn more effectively, it comes from the notion that education is something to be got out of the way, like getting a cavity filled or draining your septic tank. These are things we had just as soon not do at all, but if we have to do them it's best to get them done as quickly as possible and, then, forget about them.

I used to get that feeling when I attended board meetings where there was quite a bit of posturing about how a man needed to get his education behind him so he could get on with real life.

Such thoughts come from not being able to tell the difference between education and schooling, or, more likely, from not even knowing there is a difference. A mind in that state of innocence is unlikely to have had any genuine educational experiences at all.

It may be true that there's too much schooling in America right now. People seem to be driving themselves crazy over it, if for no other reason than not knowing how to pay for it. I saw a commercial yesterday claiming that by 2002 education on the web is going to be a two billion dollar business. I suppose that makes some folks salivate thinking how they can get their share of the two billion. But such people, of course, aren't thinking about education. They don't know what it is. What they're thinking about is selling degrees, or certificates, or credentials of some sort, and jamming people deeper into debt than they're in already.

Education isn't a business. It's a process of life, and as such it needs to go on as long as life goes on. Just think about it: you hardly ever hear a guy say that he's going to live till he's eighty years old but he's going to stop eating when he's forty. That's because he knows that in order to live he's got to eat. But what most people don't know is that in order to live well they have to educate themselves—every day. That's what we need to be teaching our students, and not just by preaching abstractions but by showing them, without any doubt, why and how it's true.

The prime message that ought to be delivered through a course of university study is that education is just as vital to human life as eating, and drinking, and doing sex, and defecating. And if that message isn't delivered then no other message will be worth much. My sense is that the university scarcely ever thinks about the value of its messages. Gore Vidal, in one of his essays, remarked that the principal effect of taking a course from a typical English professor is to induce a determination never again to read a poem or a novel. I'm afraid that's too often true, and it shows just how confused about education the academy is. Education is generally regarded as something to be got, and once got, stored away in a seldom-visited vault. One of the saddest scenes I've observed is students lining up at a college bookstore to sell back the books from completed courses. A book to be sold back is a book that never should have been acquired in the first place because nothing of worth was got from it. It is better not to take a course than to take it and then never think of its subject matter again. In the latter case, the course has served as an inoculation against thought, which Eugene Victor Walter once said is the goal of undergraduate education as it is now conducted.

The habit of thinking of education as outside the normal stream of life, outside *everydayness*, has created the damnable notion that the purpose of liberal learning is to provide a smattering of culture. It is presumably a good thing for a banker, for example, on those occasions when he turns his attention away from gouging money out of people, to know that Proust wrote *Remembrance of Things Past* or that Adam Smith was the author of *Wealth of Nations*. Why it's a good thing I've never been able to figure. If the effect of liberal learning is merely to produce a veneer of smoothness, then we would do better without it. It's far safer to take your predators pure; then, at least, you have no illusions about them.

Within the university, this kind of culture-buggery serves to bring out two nominally opposed groups who actually are less opposed to each other than each is to education itself. On the one hand you have men of practical mind who have no time for aesthetic crap because they're, as they say incessantly, "concentrated on the bottom line." On the other, you have professorial aesthetes, who are proud of their inability to do simple arithmetic, and who claim to be enthralled by the higher things of life without ever getting around to saying what they are. If the fate of the university lies in the outcome of the debate between these two, then it doesn't matter how it turns out. Education is banished before the argument gets underway.

Martin Heidegger, when preparing to return to his home university after a four-year stint away, teaching at Marburg, wrote in November 1928 to his friend Karl Jaspers and said, "Freiburg for me will once more be a test of whether anything of philosophy is left there or whether it has all turned into learnedness." Later in life he made the same point by noting that "conceptual hairsplitting can be done from nine to five without ruffling one's suit-coat, but real philosophy demands a change in one's very existence." If we understand that Heidegger was defining philosophy as essential response to life, it would be hard to find more apt short descriptions of the battle for the soul of the university. Is it to be a place where minds are brought alive and stimulated to think? Or is it to be a place where a placid surface facade is pasted on and people are taught to content themselves with "learnedness"? Do we read our books because they are our cherished companions, and because in conversation with them we learn how to be who we are, and how to do what we're supposed to do? Or do we read them because we want to display them as badges of accomplishment, and publish articles about them, and so on? Do we wear education every day, or it is something we put on only on Sunday to go out and strut around?

I recall once sitting on the lawn in the late afternoon sun with my friend Ed Banfield (who died last fall at his summer home in East Montpelier). Ed was a man who wore his education in everyday ways as faithfully as anyone I've ever known. Since he was a professor at Harvard he caused me to wonder whether the elite institutions really do gather to them a large percentage of people who understand what education is and integrate it into their daily lives. So, I asked him. I said it had been my fate always to work in middling institutions where most of the people I had met were not committed to an educated life and I was curious whether things were different in the Harvards and Yales of the world. He answered that there were many bright, intellectually energetic people at Harvard, but that I mustn't think it was a wonderland. Then he added that in his estimation not even half of retired Harvard professors continued reading in their fields. Why not? I asked. No profit in it, he said.

I went home that night feeling better about the lot I had drawn in life.

The main reason it's going to take quite a few letters for me even to begin to get straight what I'm trying to say is that language plays tricks on us. Words present themselves in one guise in one setting and, then, almost as opposite things in another. I've spoken here, for example, of "culture" in disparaging tones. But I know there are ways of speaking in which culture becomes a fine thing. Here's Matthew Arnold, writing in the preface to *Literature and Dogma*:

> To understand that the language of the Bible is fluid, passing, and literary, not rigid, fixed, and scientific, is the first step towards the right understanding of the Bible. But to take this very first step, some experience of how men have thought and expressed themselves, and some flexibility of spirit, are necessary; and this is culture.

If this is culture, then I'm all for it. All the same, we still have to ask how a person achieves experience of the thinking and expression of others, and how a person assumes a flexibility of spirit. We can't paste these things onto ourselves by rote learning. They can't be drilled into us by task masters. They have to come from open, free interaction with good minds. And the habit of seeking, everyday, open, free interaction with good minds is education.

I harp on the *everydayness* of this not only because it's essential, but because I'm up against a vast social misconception which holds that education is something which occurs only in special settings and usually has to be accompanied by the payment of substantial fees. The portion of the university world focused on degree-selling is afraid of the truth that education can occur anywhere honest minds interact. But, this is a misplaced fear. If the degree-sellers understood the proper function of the university, they could admit that it is merely the servant of education, not its proprietor. But, then, they could go on to argue that the university is a place designed specifically to encourage free, open, candid interaction. Right now they seek for gimmicks because they don't think this is enough. That's because they have no faith in what the university is supposed to do.

The medieval Dominican thinker Meister Eckhart said, "Those who are not of a great essence, whatever work they perform, nothing comes of it." The only genuine essence the university has is education, and those who are not of it can flounder around from morning to night in incessant busy-work, and ten years hence there will be no trace of what they did.

My response to anyone who questions whether we should spend as much time as we do on education is to ask in return:

Are we fanatical to think of eating everyday?

Are we fanatical to think of drinking everyday?

Are we fanatical to have fantasies of pleasure everyday?

If the answer is no, then neither is it fanatical to try to educate ourselves everyday, and to wonder continually about how it might be done better. The good of future eating, drinking, and pleasure depends on educating ourselves, as do lots of other important things.

I'm not sure it was necessary to write this letter. Maybe everything I've said here has been obvious. But I thought it would be well to answer in advance possible critics who might say we're over-doing this discussion. I don't see that an activity essential to decent human life which is currently talked about mostly as something other than what it is, can, at the moment, be overdone. With that in mind, I'll keep on writing. But not today.

Of all words in English, the one that is most often used to mean the opposite of what it actually means is "practicality." Explaining why that's the case was my purpose in this letter.

*I*N THIS SIXTH letter I'll try to wind up the introductory portion of the series so that from here on I can concentrate on specific features of teaching and learning. But, the introduction won't be complete without one more point about idealism and its interaction with educational practice.

I can imagine that readers of these letters might be saying that though they employ a plausible tone, they're actually so remote from the practicalities of running a university they can have little impact on ordinary, everyday behavior. It's pleasant to have an ideal but, after all, the world prescribes its realities to us, and if we don't attend to them as they exist any idealism will be futile. In the average university, most students care little for the sort of self-awakening I've been describing as education, and they can't be persuaded to care. They come to us hoping first to get credentials and second to acquire some practical skills that will help them towards employment and a competitive edge.

This is taken to be the practical stance on education, and though it is, in truth, so wildly impractical as to be insane, it maintains its force because of a false metaphor that has been planted deep in the psyche of our materialistic, secularized society. And, what is this metaphor? It's the notion of social reality as a rational machine which admittedly exhibits a few kinks and rattles from time to time but which, for the most part, supports human aspirations in a benign and sensible way. Consequently, the first job for all of us is to transform ourselves into efficient cogs for the machine so that it will incorporate us amiably and so that we can help it grind away happily. And, if we'll do this, then all things will be as they should be. It was this vision a former president of my university had in mind when he would say, as he did frequently, "The first thing they've gotta learn is that everybody's gotta have a boss!"

An early lesson of education is that there is no such machine. All history tells us there is no such machine, and that there never can be one. If it were possible, it would long since have been put in place, and its cheery whirring would have smoothed away the sort of dyspeptic groucheries I'm engaging in here.

What people take for the workings of the machine are actually countless human decisions rendered day by day under the influence of past education. These decisions strike us as machine-like habits because we've forgotten how they got put in place. They didn't happen by accident. Somebody, some time in the past, summoned idealism to bring them into being. Of all stupidities, the saddest is the belief that the great stratum of educated, humane decision-making is maintenance free, that once put in place it'll just sit there and work forever.

There are plenty of instances reported in the newspapers everyday to show that it doesn't work for a lot of people, and the only reason people believe in it as much as they do is that it is mostly reported on by people for whom it is, temporarily and speciously, working. Americans tend to believe that they're exempt from the horrors of history. What need have they of education when nothing really bad can happen? The worst fate imaginable is to be forced, for a few years, to take a job at K-Mart. Seldom has there been a society allowed to ride so unconsciously on the shoulders of giants.

The affliction of most so-called practical-minded men is that they believe they can escape the probings of human consciousness. They know that there are such things as religion, and philosophy, and literature, and art, all of which are devoted to discovering meaning, but they have got it in their heads that they don't have to pay attention to them. They think they can get through life without facing the human condition. And how can they do it? By keeping busy. As Pascal said, such men desire desperately to be diverted from thinking of what they are. I wish I could take them and rub their faces in my father's death, who made the same idiotic attempt, and then ask them how smart they think they are.

George Eliot captured them pretty accurately in *Middlemarch*, where she commented:

> For in the multitude of middle-aged men who go about their voca-
> tions in a daily course determined for them much in the same way
> as the tie of their cravats, there is always a good number who once
> meant to shape their own deeds and alter the world a little. The
> story of their coming to be shapen after the average and fit to be
> packed by the gross, is hardly ever told even in their consciousness;
> for perhaps their ardour in generous unpaid toil cooled as imper-
> ceptibly as the ardour of other youthful loves, until one day their
> earlier self walked like a ghost in its old home and made the new
> furniture ghastly.

What's practical about making the world you walk around in ghastly? I've never been able to figure that out.

A signal feature of the problem we face in higher education is the leader-ship of the institutions that are supposed to setting ideals in front of stu-dents. The people who regularly appear on platforms at graduation exer-cises, decked out in flowing robes, resplendent hoods, and floppy hats, are often the exact opposite of what they seek to symbolize. In actuality, they are the bland trying to lead the blander. In a column back in 1983, Lewis Lapham, the editor of *Harper's Magazine*, noted:

> Among university presidents the impulse toward outspoken ex-
> pression has become so rare that Ernest L. Boyer, president of the
> Carnegie Foundation for the Advancement of Teaching, recently

was moved to observe that he could think of only two or three prominent educators willing to violate the bounds of platitude.

Boyer must have traveled widely to have met that many.

A continuous whinery of dull-minded people is that idealists are unaware of the world's realities, that they've retreated to a never-never land where the brutal features of existence can't be acknowledged. There may, indeed, be a few starry-eyed people in that condition. I've run into some of them myself from time to time. But I see nothing idealistic about them; they are just dumb. A genuine idealist holds to his ideals precisely because he is so consistently aware of what's really going on. He knows he is surrounded by a brutal world and he wants to lessen its brutality.

It's obvious, for example, that the middling universities will draw multitudes of students with minds so coarse and tastes so low that, at the point of entry, they can't thrill to a philosophic idea, can't respond to beauty, can't imagine any form of transcendence. So what? Does that mean we give in to them and serve them up what they think they want? Some of them may be in a state so educationally degraded they can't be reached even by the most energetic teaching. But we don't know that they are until we try. For whatever it's worth, my experience has been that a majority of students will respond positively to the belief expressed by their teachers that they can learn and that they can understand. I wish I could get every member of boards of trustees to meet with Ralph Relation, a recent graduate, and listen to him speak about what happened in his own life as a result of taking a seminar on Shakespeare in the Adult Degree Program, and other experiences of that kind, which, when he enrolled, he hadn't imagined having.

We need a stronger understanding of what's actually happening when we surrender to people who claim to be promoting practicality rather than idealism in education. We need to face the world they're trying to foist on us. I talked a bit about Saul Bellow in my last letter, and it reminded me of a remark he put into the mouth of his protagonist in an earlier novel, *The Dean's December*:

And it isn't the Grand Inquisitor's universal anthill that we have to worry about after all, but something worse, more Titanic—universal stupefaction, a Saturnian, wild, gloomy, murderousness, the raging of irritated nerves, and intelligence reduced by metal poison, so that the main ideas of mankind die out, including of course the idea of freedom.

Practicality of the sort pushed by the degree salesmen of the world is not just boring, it's hellish. That's a point I may have learned most effectively from Owen Barfield, who died about a year ago, after a very long and very productive life. Dan Noel and I went to visit him once at his little house north of Rochester. I had the previous day, in Glastonbury, bought his book, *Saving the Appearances,* and that night had read the first chapter in anticipation of the visit. Dan mentioned to him that I had started his book, whereupon he turned to me and asked , "Well, are you going to read the rest of it?" I told him I would and he said, "If you do, send me a letter and tell me what you think."

After I got home, I did send him a letter and got back from him a gracious reply, which I'm more happy to have in my files each year that passes. It was in *Saving the Appearances* that I found the following passage which I think contains one of the most important truths of life:

> The relationship between the mind and heart of man is a delicate mystery, and hardness is catching. It will, I believe, be found that there is a valid connection, at some level however deep, between what I have called "literalness" and a certain hardness of heart. Listen attentively to the response of a dull or literal mind to what insistently presents itself as allegory or symbol, and you may detect a certain irritation, a faint, incipient aggressiveness in its refusal. Here I think is a deep-down moral gesture.

In another of Barfield's books, *Poetic Diction,* he points out that the struggle for education will not be won overnight:

Between those for whom "knowledge" means ignorant but effective power, and those for whom the individual imagination is the medium of all knowledge from perception upward, a truce will not readily be struck.

I fear that the dominant goal of learning at most universities is based on the notion of acquiring tools which can be used to shape the world in accordance with the student's own will. But, once we state the notion, we see how fatuous it is. People who think of education that way have no business shaping the world. They have no right to do it. And why not? Because they're not wise enough. They haven't done the fundamental work of shaping themselves, and so they continue to thrash and flounder, befouling the world with immature ego.

A prominent bromide of practicality is the adage: if you can't beat 'em, join 'em. It's too much followed in the world. But if it's followed in education, we lose everything that counts. It's not likely there will ever be a secure victory over those who are irritated by the imagination and want simply, as they say, to keep everyone's nose to business. But, as far as I'm concerned, they have to be fought even if one finds himself single and isolated. We should always remember Isaiah:

> I looked: there was no one to help me;
> I was appalled but could find no supporter!
> Then my own arm came to my rescue
> and my own fury supported me. (63:5)

Besides, things don't need to be quite that bleak. We can always go back to Saul Bellow, and hope: "Well, you can never tell what conclusions a man might reach when you try especially hard to talk straight to him."

This is the end of my general introduction. From now on I'll try to be more specific.

Until next time.

In this letter I introduced the point that's hardest to make from within the educational establishment: when you're dealing with a system decayed at the core, you're not likely to resurrect it intelligently by accepting the current organizational structure.

I PROMISED TO fling myself outside the placid precincts of introduction into the briar patch of specifics. The problem is that in briar patches we encounter unruly beasts who resist being herded into corrals. How can one find categories to contain them?

The difficulty of organizing talk about education is one reason people are reluctant to engage in it. It's easier to discuss subjects like sociology or psychology which come equipped with their own classifications. But education is a wild domain which no one has mapped adequately. I don't mind going in there, but if I get a bit lost, I don't want you to get mad at me. Remember, I have no charts in hand.

The common attempts fail because they aren't daring enough. They long for the security of formula. Yet, a truth about education is that it is essentially nonformulaic. It requires a readiness to live with uncertainty. One has to go where there are no paths. In fact, you might say that if you're on the path, you aren't getting educated. Going down the path takes neither thought nor decision; it just takes putting one foot in front of the other.

I've said, during occasional delusions of cynicism, that university professors are the most uneducable creatures you can find. That's because they are the offspring of formula, and many of them appear to have become the embodiment of formula. They identify themselves with some theory or other, and then vested interest takes over and sweeps them along the road to academic paradise, or, as we say more soberly, tenure. I was speculating, just last fall, about this process in my own little corner of the academy, and if I may be permitted to plagiarize myself, I'll copy what I wrote in my journal then:

> The coming of developmentalism to the fore of educational thinking is one of the more curious sequences of events I've observed over my lifetime. Why and how it has happened ought to be questions of intense inquiry. Yet among many of my colleagues it is accepted in the way biblical inerrancy is accepted by fundamentalist Christians. Their march to the drumbeat of developmentalism makes me wonder if it should be declared the official religion of our college. If it were, we could then engage in the pleasure of hunting down heretics, which among academics is the sport of ecstasy.

The point I'm hoping to make with this ramble is that we can't hope to organize our discussion of education by relying on the taxonomies of knowledge employed by current universities. Education is a thing for all time and not solely a creature of the strained and neurotic generation in which we find ourselves. To talk about it as though it were a package made up of the academic disciplines is like identifying Christianity with Christendom, that is, putting a parody in place of the real thing. The disciplines are not so much a part of the history of knowledge as they are an element in the history of politics. That universities commonly attempt to meet the needs of general education by so-called distribution requirements shows how politicized the system has become. Requirements are not put in place to support an educational plan; they're imposed out of attempts to maintain political peace among the departments. Without them, many of the departments would fade away, and consequently they are desperate to maintain rules that deliver freshmen and sophomore students to them independent of educational justification.

I'm not arguing that the current disciplines are perfectly efficient barriers to education. The human mind longs for it, even when it doesn't understand itself, and as a consequence some education slips through the most jargon-laden formulas. I suspect that even students of psychological developmentalism learn a little something worthwhile, although to justify it on the basis of what it delivers would be like living with a car hitting on two cylinders because it can limp down the road at twelve miles an hour.

Truth is, the academic disciplines have almost no interest in education. What they are, at their best, are networks created to produce certain sorts of books. The majority of these books are worthless. But not all. Some of them rise to the level of explaining intelligently how the formulas of the disciplines can complement thought. A complement to thought, however, is not thought itself because it lacks the personalized insight that thought requires. Still, that's no reason to be down on it so long as it presents itself for what it is: a tool rather than a thing of plenary value.

A person like yourself, schooled in the applications of science, needs to remember that many of the university's concerns are not as well-grounded as the curriculum which was taught to you. It's not easy to decide whether the typical university promotes more educational activity or more that falls in the category of miseducation. At any given time the catalogues of universities will be littered with subjects that subsequent eras will discover to have been trash. It wasn't all that long ago that society was being enlightened by professors of phrenology and racial science. We can pray that the gurus of management theory, gender-ethics counseling, and sexual-encounter hermeneutics will shortly meet the fate these charlatans did a century ago. But, in the meantime, they are gobbling up students and leading them down the primrose path. Education is supposed to protect them against these academic predators, but if they meet no one who knows what education is, where will their defenses come from? The degree-salesmen have no interest in answering because a degree purchased for learning pretentious rubbish is paid for in the same dollars as one leading to a beginning mastery of physics. And, dollars, as we know, pave the bottom line.

In Thomas Hardy's *Under the Greenwood Tree,* a group of villagers are discussing the decision of the new rector to replace the traditional string mu-

sic during church services with a new-fangled organ. One of the former
choir members remarks:

> Then the music is second to the woman, the other churchwarden is
> second to Shinar, the pa'son is secondary to the churchwardens,
> and God A'Mighty is nowhere at all.

You don't have to know the details of the novel to see that he's talking
about the common human propensity to put secondary things ahead of the
primary. The universities are doing that, and what with careerism, worship
of success, professionalism, degree-salesmanship, an insane obsession with
competition, and bottom line-ism, education is nowhere at all. There's a
value in secondary things so long as education is around to help one figure
out what to do with them. But, take education away and these things are
little better than pitch-penny.

I've gone a long way round to explain why it would be foolish to talk about
the specifics of education as they're usually discussed. Doing that would be
to fall into the trap I want to escape. Yet, it's easier to know how to stay out
of bad places than to get into good ones. Since I have no interest in becoming, like the functionaries of the Circumlocution Office, an expert in how
not to do it, I'm left with the problem of organizing the specifics of real
education. And I'm not perfectly sure I can. All I can do is try to push
through my own intellectual weakness. It'll be a blundering process, but
when you're lost it's either blunder or lie down and die.

In the midst of confusion one has to find something to hold onto and build
out from as a base. As I was sitting here asking what my anchor might be,
my eye fell on a little box of stationery whose lid is imprinted with a comment from Daphne du Maurier: "Happiness is not a possession to be prized;
it is a quality of thought, a state of mind." It reminded me that when you're
puzzled the best thing to do is open your eyes. If happiness is not a possession, neither is education. You can't unscrew the top of anybody's head and
pour it in, as though you were slopping the hogs. Education is a way of
looking at the world, and one gets to where he can look at it in an educated

way only through persistent effort. This being the case, specifics might be approached by discussing particular efforts required to attain an educated perspective. In any case, that's the best I can do at the moment. So for at least the next several letters I'm going to direct my attention to the habits of education and how to weave them into the self.

I strolled down to the Bear Pond Bookshop this morning, as I often do when I'm in a state of befuddlement, and browsed through a copy of Wendell Berry's new essay, *Life Is A Miracle.* In the first chapter, Berry makes the point that to reduce life to human understanding is to enslave it. He reminded me that the primary habit of the educated mind, the one without which the others are unlikely to follow, is a willingness to live with uncertainty. Nothing holds one away from education more effectively than a determination to get everything settled. If people want to settle everything, they will, and then there's no more room left for learning because they think they know everything.

At some time during every semester, I find it necessary to remind my students of the wonderful remark Keats made in a letter he wrote to his brothers on December 21, 1817. He was twenty-two at the time. It was a striking insight for a person that young.

> At once it struck me what quality went to form a Man of Achievement, especially in Literature, and which Shakespeare possessed so enormously— I mean Negative Capability, that is, when a man is capable of being in uncertainties, mysteries, doubts, without any irritable reaching after fact and reason....

When I find a student with developed negative capability, I know my teaching job is going to be easy. And when I find one without a trace of it, then I know it's going to be like pulling eye-teeth and there's a good chance I'm going to fail. Among the hundreds of students I've had over the years, I've had only four who struck me as being positively evil. And not a one of them could begin to imagine what negative capability is.

The stance taken by most educators about qualities of this sort, which they may recognize as desirable but which aren't amenable to being charted, is to hope for them but not to work for them. That's a mistake. If the ability to be continuously aware that one can't know everything, and the understanding that there are factors bearing on every issue which one has not been able to take into account, is required for genuine learning, then it should be taught as a fundamental of education. And it shouldn't be professed only as an abstraction. About every thesis a student submits, she should be asked: what do you not know about this that might change your mind about it? There's too little mind-changing in education nowadays, and that may be because the professors themselves are often lacking in negative capability.

I know this is a simple point with which to start my list of specifics. But simple or not it's important. Too often we shy away from making points because we think they're commonly understood. But what's commonly understood is commonly forgotten. In any endeavor there's no substitute for incessant return to fundamentals and this is even more true of education than it is of other activities. So if over my next several letters I say what everybody knows I make no apology for it. Everyone may know it; but it's for sure that everybody's not applying it. And that's the problem with our lackadaisical schooling.

I'm at the end of this, and being there, I'll stop.

THE EIGHTH LETTER

At this point, I struck a more personal note than in any other of these missives. I could have left it out of this edition, but since the incident it relates was a part of putting the letters together, I decided to include it. Though it changed slightly my use of time it was of no significance in shaping my thought.

I'M SORRY TO have gone this long without sending a letter. As you know, I've been to England, squiring people around to places connected to Thomas Hardy and Jane Austen. The tour went well, and the part of it that was most satisfying for me was seeing people with busy lives turn their minds to literature in a manner that showed they understand why the aesthetics of life do require our attention—that is, if we are to be sensible men and women.

I got a call from the director of the Adult Degree Program this morning telling me I would not be included in the teaching staff this year. It wasn't unexpected. You know as well as I that letters of this sort don't curry favor with bureaucrats. The director, of course, assured me that the letters had nothing to do with the decision. It was just a matter of student numbers. He even complimented me on the quality of my teaching. Like other officials of his ilk, he's an expert in masking motives. But, that an association which has lasted thirty-two years should be severed on the first opportunity after the letters commenced at least raises a question. It's a minor point in institutional history, and people will believe what they will about it.

The good feature of the severance—though I won't deny that I regret it—is that I can go forward with these letters more rapidly than I intended, and, perhaps, get through the entire thirty-six by early next year.

You'll recall that in our presence about a month ago another erstwhile director complimented me on the critical acuity of my comments but suggested they had little of positive character that could guide anyone towards specific pedagogical practice. Though I suspect he conceives of practice as fairly mechanical process—an attitude induced by his, as yet, insufficient recovery from directorism—I took his remark to heart and resolved to concentrate more directly than I had previously intended on actions one can take to educate himself. I don't fancy this will satisfy my critics. They, for the most part, have not imagined that education exists. Consequently, actions taken to move toward it will continue to strike them as either unreal or, just as bad, things to which units of measurement can't be assigned. I can't help that. I'm writing about education, and not about things the degree salesmen find it easy to package and hawk. They, of course, want to tack the name of education onto their goods, but that's a matter for them and Gabriel, or St. Peter, or whomever they will meet at the Pearly Gates. One can't spend his entire life trying to talk to people who can't imagine the thing being talked about.

Since the material of education is the self (and not things that can be done to other selves), it requires at its core an evolving vision. The wondrous, and maddening, quality of this vision is that you can never, completely, pin it down. I recall another official of the university who used to brag regularly that he had accomplished everything in life he wanted to accomplish. I don't doubt that this was so. But it proves beyond question that education was not among his aspirations. We don't accomplish education; we live it, and though we can live it with sincerity and determination, we can't live it perfectly.

In Tennyson's famous poem about the aging Ulysses, the old warrior says:

> Yet all experience is an arch wherethrough
> Gleams that untravelled world, whose margin fades
> For ever and for ever when I move.

The poet was writing about a figure renowned throughout Western history for his inventiveness and eagerness to learn. He should be juxtaposed with others who don't want to move, who never step through that arch towards the untravelled world or towards a vision of the self who is competent to sojourn there. Hard as it is to believe, there are people who go years on end without asking themselves who they want to be as they approach the end of their span. There's nothing more miseducative than being obsessed by what one wants to get but never attending to who one wants to be.

Every now and then I ask my students (I have to get in the habit now of saying, "I used to ask my students") a series of questions such as:

> Do you want to die without having read Charles Dickens?
> Do you want to die without understanding the basic arguments of Immanuel Kant?
> Do you want to die without having discussed with somebody Plato's Parable of the Cave?
> Do you want to die without having memorized a poem by Wordsworth?
> Do you want to die without ever having solved a differential equation?
> Do you want to die without knowing the order of battle at Trafalgar?

Their response is interesting. They generally appear startled, as though no one had ever asked them such questions before, and as though they had never given thought to the transformative experiences they need to have. It makes me wonder what their former teachers have been doing?

Dr. Johnson is famous for having asked:

> Must helpless Man, in Ignorance sedate,
> Swim darkling down the Current of his fate?

The answer, clearly, is yes, unless one has a vision of self, to be prayed for, and struggled towards, and shaped to the best of his ability. To know that one must have that vision, and be guided towards it by whatever spiritual assistance he can summon, is the first practical requirement of education, because without it, no education is possible. Not even a first step can be taken.

You would think, wouldn't you, that if a thing is so essential to a process that the process can't be begun without it, that it would be given attention and respect by the supposed mentors of that process? Yet, the practical men, the degree-salesmen, the career-mongers, who puff themselves incessantly as the great managers of education, never mention the task of aesthetic self-formation. When something that fundamental is systematically ignored, its want can't be attributed to absent-mindedness. There's a will at work, and in this case it's a will for turning students into fodder for the mastications of the material, economic world. A good many university managers are engaged in nothing more than constructing feeding troughs for the powers that be. Benedict Arnold, Quisling, and Judas were pikers beside these guys.

I picked up Harold Bloom's latest book at the Bear Pond last week and have begun to work my way through it. It's titled *How To Read and Why*, and it interests me particularly because the activity he calls reading has many parallels with the activity I am calling education. The difference, of course, is that genuine reading involves learning from books whereas education involves learning from life (life, incidentally, in which books normally play a significant part). The one is a broader and more inclusive version of the other, yet the intelligent approaches to both are similar.

Bloom bases his book on an argument that is powerful, but also very dangerous. If I can spell out its appeal and its perils, that should be enough to finish off this letter and complete my point that a vision of self is an essential, and the first, demand of authentic education. Bloom says that the pleasures of reading are selfish, not social, that the solitary reader reads for himself. Then he goes on to punctuate his stance with this remark: "I am wary of any arguments whatsoever that connect the pleasures of solitary reading to the public good."

Though, at bottom, I disagree with him, I understand why he's pushing the issue so hard. He has seen the elite universities partially captured by ideologues, people who want to use great works of literature to advance petty "isms" of one sort or another. These are the sort of scholars who attempt to make Jane Austen relevant by turning her into a proto-feminist. I think Bloom should take a lesson from Jane Austen and be more ready to laugh at them than he is. We don't have to worry about her; she can take care of herself. She will continue to delight common readers long after the dogmatists who are trying to leech onto her now have been scraped off like barnacles from a ship in dry dock.

Still, I understand Bloom's frustration. Ideological critics insult literature in the same fashion the degree-salesmen insult education. And, as you've noticed, I'm not perfect in following my own advice to laugh at them (though I have to admit when I step back from the process that they are comical). The reason neither Bloom nor I can laugh as heartily as perhaps we ought is that though, over the long run, literature and education can take care of themselves, in the short term students are being damaged by these intellectual slugs. It's infuriating to see time that might be spent helping students towards real education diverted to ignoble ends. It's excruciatingly infuriating to watch students with potentially good minds and active imaginations being shuffled down the path to intellectual sluggism themselves, and to face the truth that the blank rounds currently in charge have the power to do it. Still, the world is as it is. We have to live in it, and hope and pray that it can find the power to illuminate itself. And this is where the danger of Bloom's position arises.

By arguing that reading is for the self alone, that it can convey no social benefit, Bloom offers ammunition to those who dismiss reading and real education as mere effete self-indulgence. "What's the good of all this crap?" thunder the practical minds of our culture who want everyone to get down to the business of selling and buying more insurance policies. We have to be careful not to do anything to aid those voices. They've already turned vast stretches of American life into a wasteland, and if they have their way, they'll transform every university into cogs for their machine, aided pre-

sumably by the promise of the internet which will do away with the ineffi-
ciency of face-to-face dialogue.

Bloom does, I confess, without really admitting it, turn back on himself by
quoting Emerson approvingly to this effect: "A scholar is a candle which
the love and desire of all men will light."

If by reading, and by educating ourselves, and by pursuing an aesthetic vision of the self, we can turn ourselves into candles, it seems clear that we
are affording a benefit to society, or, at least, to the kind of society
that's worth living in. The hazard of Bloom's original stance is that it may
cause some of us to view society continually as the enemy, as a thing to be
escaped from in order to find the pleasures of individual life. But if we try
only to escape, we leave society in the hands of those who will turn it
into pure mechanism. Maybe readers can do that, but educated people
cannot. The latter are required to pursue both the redeemed person and a
redeemed world.

In the end, the proposition of education is simple. Society is made up of
people, and since it is, we are forced to asked ourselves what kind of people
we want to be around. When we walk into a room, do we hope to find an
array of candles or a pack of slugs? And that depends on who we, ourselves,
want to be. Slugs, I guess, like to glob up together, stuck so close you can't
tell where one ends and another starts.

Another two thousand words, and another stretch of a few days before you
get another letter.

I'm not sure when I learned this, but for a number of years I've known that a person's attitude toward time is one of the most important things about him. Here, I wanted to show something of how this attitude interacts with education.

*T*ODAY I'LL CONTINUE with my list of specific practicalities, while keeping in mind that they won't strike the degree salesmen as practical at all. In letters seven and eight, I talked about staying aware that our knowledge is both incomplete and insufficient, and about the need for developing a personal vision of self. Now, I'll try to sketch out a relationship to time that complements those first two.

My friend Ed Banfield in his book *The Unheavenly City* argued that the only significant definition of class turns on the amount of time a person is willing to take into account. The highest classes are those who see themselves as immersed in history and eager to apply the lessons of the past to the problems of the future. The lowest classes are those who can take no more than the next hour into account and concentrate their thoughts on it alone. I'm not sure if this is a perfect way to think about social class, but when we come to the class structures of education, it's powerfully accurate.

I once asked the students in a class I was teaching the following question:

> Does time obliterate suffering, so that after the passage of years it really doesn't matter any more? Can you feel sympathy for Roman parents whose child died in a plague, or did that happen so long ago that it doesn't any longer count? If time does wipe out the significance of suffering, how long does it take?

Here are two of the answers I received:

> Too much removal to care about Roman parents whose child died in a plague. In fact most people are done feeling sorry 20 or 30 minutes after hearing about a 747 airplane crash. I think that we, as a people of today, are so geared up that we don't have time to dwell on non-immediate subjects. Unless that plane had a friend or relative on it, it's of almost no concern. It's of no concern, that is, until we find ourselves boarding the next plane bound for windshear city. Then we have remembrance. Perhaps selfish, but still remembrance. Roman parents? No—no concern at all.

> I believe that time doesn't obliterate suffering. If a person close to you dies, then time will never make the pain and suffering go away. I as a person feel anguish for all who have died an unnecessary death throughout time. I think everyone has a little compassion within themselves for others, even the persons of long ago. Time can never heal the wounds of love and death. People over time learn to deal with it better, but never fully get over the pain.

Keep in mind that these were nineteen-year-olds who can't be expected to have formed mature views, and notice, also, that the first answer may have been informed by a becoming sarcasm. But if we take the two at face value, it seems fairly clear which writer was likely to move towards education and which might have been enrolled primarily to obtain a job certificate.

When I was a child, I thought the world was moving along a path towards something that could be called decency, or humanity, or civilization. Not only did I think it was on the path, I thought it was pretty far along the path. Just a few more steps—like the elimination of cancer and atomic bombs—I would tell myself, and then we would have reached a condition not perfect but good enough so that no one would have the right to complain of it.

I was naive in the way many young people are naive. But I may not have been completely wrong. The world may be on the path. I'm no longer sure it is, but it may be. Yet, obviously, if it is, it's not as far along as I thought it was. It seems to me now we are at least five hundred years short of where I thought we were in 1950.

What is one to do when he discovers in the midst of a journey that he is five hundred years behind where he thought he was?

He could lie down and cry. It would be understandable upon finding that one cannot reach in his lifetime the point he thought he had already attained. There's hardly anything more discouraging than learning that something one has hoped for and thought he was working towards is beyond any possibility of personal achievement.

This, of course, is exactly the condition Moses found himself in at the end of *Deuteronomy,* when he has climbed to the top of Pisgah, across from Jericho. As you'll recall, God says to him:

> This is the land of which I swore to Abraham, to Isaac, and to Jacob, "I will give it to your descendants." I have let you see it with your eyes, but you shall not go over there.

Then, the account continues, "So Moses, the servant of the Lord, died there in the land of Moab, according to the word of the Lord."

Guess what, Dalton? We're all going to die in the land of Moab.

If we allow that thought to paralyze us, then about all we can do is lie down and cry—or surrender to an equivalent, like taking drugs, or living to play slot machines, or eating ourselves to death, or selling degrees.

Yet, as I used to tell my students, we should always return to the text. Any text worth reading can be read a number of ways, but to me it appears legitimate to find in this one the message that if you die a servant of the Lord, where you die doesn't matter all that much.

If we, as we say so foolishly, translate this into a secular context, it means that we need to take ourselves outside personal time and move into something that might be called real time. None of us can do that perfectly. As Dr. Johnson reminded us: "Tell a man he's to be hanged in a fortnight, and it concentrates his mind powerfully." Few of us are enough in real time to approach our own hanging placidly, and, yet, if we wish to live educated lives , we do need to think about the passage of time in more realistic ways than is common. We need to learn that good things come into the world more slowly than we would wish and that many of them cannot be attained in a lifetime, or a string of lifetimes. Yet, if a thing takes a thousand years, that's what it takes. Does that necessarily make it not worthwhile?

One answers in terms of who he thinks he is, in time. My argument here is that the educated life demands seeing oneself as an actor in a long series of events, each one of which will continue to exercise influence throughout time. This, I realize, is a strange notion in the cut-and-slash world of the present. But without it, there is nothing to stop people from grabbing incessantly at whatever is in front of their faces, leaving human interaction to resemble a pack of pigs at the trough.

I've been reading an intriguing book by the Oxford historian Theodore Zeldin titled *An Intimate History of Humanity.* He makes a point similar to the one I'm making by saying:

> Most people, without realizing it, still perpetuate the habits of mind they have inherited from the days when it was expected that the world would come to an end very soon, and have not learned to view it as having infinite possibilities. Pessimism and optimism thus emerge as being a dispute, to a great extent, about how far one is prepared to look, about focal distances.

He's right about the pessimism. People, if asked, would deny being pessimists. Yet, their behavior tells us how profoundly gloomy they are. It confirms the belief that a genuine enrichment of the world is impossible, so that all one is left with is the prospect of grabbing as much as possible before death puts an end not only to one's pleasures but to the total effects of one's life. This is, essentially, a brutish idea, yet it's the idea that drives the behavior of most people.

We can see it in the thrust of the modern curricula, particularly those that are most avidly advertised. The message, essentially, is this: come to us to learn how to manipulate other people so you can be sure to get yours. It's made shamelessly, as though all people who might perceive its core vulgarity have been erased from the world. And, perhaps, most of them have.

Education will never come to the center of university schooling until students are immersed in a richer, more imaginative, and more idealistic view of time than they have now. To put it bluntly, they have to start thinking about it in bigger hunks. Until they do, they will play the role society now expects of them: scarcely emancipated peasants on the make. Education doesn't care whether a person is successful, that being a matter left to other aspirations. It cares about a person's contribution to a rich evolution of time.

I try every now and then to imagine how crazy I sound to the degree salesmen, and, with respect to what I've said above, it's easy to hear them muttering about an impossible idealism that can never make any difference. That's because their "never" is bounded by five years on either side of where they are now. I was thinking of this just the other night reading in Joseph Persico's account of the Nuremberg trials of 1945-46. As the evidence of what had been done became ever more clear and ever more horrendous, a generally unspoken question seemed to rise and hover over the proceedings: what were these men thinking of to have fallen in with these outrages?

The answer is fairly simple. They were thinking that their lives would pass by before any serious changes in the power configurations would take place.

They made two bad mistakes, one to my mind far worse than the other. Actual conditions changed faster than they anticipated, so that they quickly went from strutting before cheering thousands to sitting abjectly in a dock waiting to be hanged. That was the lesser mistake. The greater was their belief that what they had done would pass away, swamped by the fame of their position, so that they would be remembered for the posts they held and not for the acts they committed. Göring predicted that within fifty years there would be statues of him all over Germany. Has there ever been quite so much misplaced faith in success?

The prison psychologist Gustave Gilbert asked Rudolf Hoess, former commandant of Auschwitz, whether the Jews had deserved to be killed. He replied: "We were all so trained to obey orders without thinking that the thought of disobeying them never occurred to anybody. I never gave much thought to whether it was wrong. It just seemed a necessity." It was an honest answer, and it shows he was thinking of necessity, *at the time*. He gave no thought to how he would be seen a century hence. An educated man would have given thought to it because he would by his nature have projected his mind beyond what was in front of his face. I'm not claiming that historical reputation is the only, or even the main, reason not to murder people. But a sense of it can work together with other decent motives to steel us when we are faced with hard decisions. That's the kind of work education must do if it's worth the name.

Over the course of my association with colleges and universities, the idea that our knowledge and wisdom must be grounded in history has faded. It needs be restored, by being integrated directly into teaching. And we need to remind ourselves that history is not just something that has happened in our own country over the past couple centuries but is the record of all people over all time, and, furthermore, that what we do right now modifies that entire record for good or for ill.

Enough for today. I'll be back soon.

The impediments to education that I began to discuss in this letter are marked by an inclination to deal only with the surface of things. It's a habit that can be defended, although the defenses I've seen haven't won me over. For one of the more intriguing, one should go to Mitchell Stephens, The Rise of the Image the Fall of the Word *(Oxford University Press, 1998).*

*T*HE NEXT THREE specifics I want to discuss are connected to what I've come to think of as the great refusals: key attitudes which cripple attempts to put education at the center of university life. These are all mixed up with one another, but in order to lay them out as clearly as I can, I'll devote a separate letter to each one.

I start with the refusal to engage in dialogue because dialogue is the core activity of an educated life and without it nothing that deserves the name can take place. Those who turn aside from it, who claim to be too busy for it, are education's most dangerous enemies.

In each generation, the opponents of education find new excuses for not being able to subject their ideas to the rigors of give and take. There is now afoot in the university world, for example, the attempt I alluded to earlier in these letters to become more efficient by streamlining the so-called delivery mechanisms. It's a movement that has been mightily stimulated by the advent of the internet and by electronic systems for sending words and pictures back and forth. And it claims to be a great boon to communication, showing once again the devil's propensity to arrive on the scene clad in the raiment of the Lord. Or, as George Herbert put it in the 670th of his *Outlandish Proverbs:* "No sooner is a temple built to God but the devil builds a chapel hard by."

This isn't to say that the internet and e-mail are always destructive of education. They're not. But most of the schemes now being put forward in the name of more efficient educational concourse aren't based on respect for dialogue. That's probably because those who are the most avid revolutionists in the attempt to electronicize everything don't know what dialogue is.

I know we shouldn't generalize too much from our own experiences because we each encounter only a tiny slice of life. Yet, I can't help observing that those I've known who are the biggest pushers of the electronic revolution are exactly the people least likely to engage in serious conversation. I'm not saying they won't chatter a lot. But they won't stick with a dialogue long enough to allow anything of significance to happen.

This isn't surprising when you think about it. A prime characteristic of people who place efficiency high on the list of virtues is nervous impatience. They're always rushing to the next place, always consulting their date books, always leaving the room to take or place a telephone call. Nearly the whole of their public facade is designed to emphasize their busy-ness. Such habits may be useful in the production and marketing of tooth-paste— business now, as you know, moves at the speed of light—but they do nothing to enhance education. There is no habit more essential to dialogue than deep patience.

I recall once, years ago, a student came to me for my last appointment of the afternoon, just before we were to go to supper. She was obviously wrought up and had a story to tell about her efforts to think through her educational course, which hadn't been going as she wished. She was frustrated. She cried a bit. When the hour was up, her story wasn't over. So I listened some more, and some more after that. We talked on until eleven o'clock, when all of a sudden she fell silent. It was as though she had had her say and had no more words at the moment. She smiled and said she had to go. So, I said okay.

A couple years after she graduated, she wrote me a letter and mentioned the evening, saying it had meant more to her than I could imagine. She had never before had the chance to chase her ideas right to the bottom, as she put it, and see, really, what they were worth.

Obviously, we can't have conversations of that length everyday. Yet, they're sometimes necessary in order for a feature of educated life to take hold. In this particular talk, what was going on was the student's attempt to get the experiences of her life into a reasoned relationship with educational ideals she had recently encountered. There was no other way for her to do it except through a kind of concentrated floundering which allowed her to decide what went where. Experiences of that kind demand the physical presence of a listener, the encouragement of a smile, small movements of the hand which say, without words, it's okay, go ahead, jokes stuck in at the right moment to offer respite, the intensity that comes from tone of voice and repositioning of the body. These are things we learn in dialogue, and without dialogue we do not learn them, not ever.

All the session required from me was a little patience, a lost supper, and missing a couple TV shows I might otherwise have watched. It was a small price to pay for helping a student get something she could get in no other way. Yet, how often are we willing to pay even that tiny price for genuine educational movement?

The necessity of dialogue for an educated life is poorly understood because modern society is organized to divert attention from the attitude that probably causes more human misery than anything else. I'm referring to what William Blake called single vision, or the locking of oneself into a prescribed perspective without the imaginative resources ever to get out. People gain relief from their problems by changing the focus of their vision, by coming to understand that there are other ways of seeing things besides the one that has them tied in knots. But, society doesn't want those knots untied. And since dialogue is the only workable means for casting off bonds of that kind, then, naturally, the social mechanism is afraid of it.

One thing we mustn't delude ourselves about is what society expects of us and how education relates to it. Genuine education is not a means of fitting smoothly into economic society—which is, of course, the degenerate notion that prevails among the degree salesmen. In the view of economic convention each of us exists as a plug that needs only to be stuffed into an existing hole. The managerial mentality doesn't concern itself with how you feel about being in the hole (unless, of course, it can use those feelings to manipulate you). It doesn't give a whit for your personal enhancement. It wants you to do what the hole requires of you, and if you don't, it's more than ready to cast you aside and find somebody to take your place.

Education, by contrast, though it is willing to give the existing system its due, is not focused on it primarily. It cares first about the educated life for individual people, and second for how those people can bring a brighter, more engaging society into existence. There can be no advance towards the latter goal until greater numbers of people learn to reason together. That's where dialogue comes in.

One reason the degree salesmen oppose dialogue is its expense. It costs money to seat inexperienced people in comfortable rooms, in small enough groups that they can talk to one another, and leave them there with a teacher long enough for them to come to know their own thoughts and to learn how to express themselves. There is no better way to promote education. Humanity has known this for a very long time. Yet the degree salesmen, with education well below the top of their priority list and selling certificates at the pinnacle, are continually trying to convince their customers that cheaper, shoddier, ways are superior. So long as they are what they are—salesmen rather than educators—they'll continue trying to sell inferior services packaged as something so up-to-date it puts past practice to shame.

It wouldn't be hard for university leaders, if they were genuinely devoted to education, to turn their minds towards educational solutions to their financial problems. But since most of them have little personal involvement in education, the thought doesn't occur.

I wish endemic cheapness were the only barrier to inserting dialogue into the core of university life. If it were, the task of gaining the attention of administrators would be easier than it is. Financially supportable plans for dialogue could be proposed. The results of strong teaching could be demonstrated. And if one kept hammering at these, over time, movement might begin.

I'm not saying that cheapness by itself isn't an exacting foe. I've watched it work for a long time and seen it carry numerous battles. It has a lot going for it, including its seeming rootedness in the human soul. Yet, I suspect it could be held in check within the university were it not allied with a force stronger than itself: unconscious intellectual cowardice.

You may be saying, "Hell, John, if cheapness is sunk in deep, cowardice is at the very core of the beast. If we have to get rid of it to support education we might as well give up and go home."

It's a strong argument, and I confess I think about giving up everyday. But when I reflect on what I'd be giving up to, I have to put the thought aside. Besides, I don't think the situation is as hopeless as outward conditions indicate.

University culture, after all, is simply a rear-guard manifestation of national culture. And, lately, there have been signs that the anti-intellectualism, or anti-thoughtfulness, heralded by a long stream of American social historians is waning. There are more bookstores, there are more reading clubs, there are more lectures than there were forty years ago. We now have a cable channel that does nothing but talk about books throughout the weekend. Even national political leaders who cannot be imagined ever to have read a serious book try to pretend that they have. Or they appoint advisors who feed them book titles along with snippets of things to say about them. Much of this is simply posturing, but we need to keep in mind William James's teaching that reality follows pretense. If it's true that acting happy will make you happy, maybe pretending to have read a book will lead on, some day, actually to having read one.

Till now, none of this has had much effect on university practice, especially not among the leadership. Yet, even in those stolid precincts, there may be cause for hope, and it comes from the characteristic that up till now has been extremely depressing. American university leadership is perfectly conventional. If the culture signals them that they're supposed to be two-fisted, hard-nosed, practical, no-nonsense, kick-ass financial managers, then that's exactly what they'll try to be. But, if the signals change, you'll see them turning around overnight.

The other feature of the situation that offers hope is the truth that intellectual fearfulness is unconscious among most university people. They don't know that they avoid dialogue because they're afraid. If we can bring their motives into consciousness and make clear that their unwillingness comes from their being fearful and not because they're too busy to get around to it, then, at least, they would be forced to make a bow towards the exchange and examination of ideas. And right now, given how they have been behaving, even a bow would be wonderful.

All this tells me that dialogue, pursued wherever the opportunity arises, has some chance of turning the university towards education and away from salesmanship. I don't suppose it matters whether reform comes from within or from the outside as long as the stultifying behavior is shaken.

I see that I've reached my limit without saying as much as I had intended about how dialogue stimulates thinking on specific subjects. But since we have many letters to go, I'll get back to that someday. Next time, though, I'll move on to the second of the great refusals.

You can observe a lust for simplemindedness in every bar and barbershop in the land. What most people don't know is that the same lust, in a slightly gussied-up form, dominates the universities as well.

*O*N TO THE second of the great refusals. This one I have more sympathy for than the refusal to engage in dialogue because it seems to reflect a universal tendency in mankind, one we all have to struggle against if we want to honor education. I'm speaking of the inclination to pretend that things are less complex than they are and, consequently, to make claims based on insufficient knowledge. Though I recognize that it's an impulse wired into us, I'm also forced to admit that it causes as much harm as intellectual cowardice does. Jacques Barzun is right to say that all great errors of the mind come from reason working upon fragments of experience.

I was reminded of this forcefully last night when I went to a public forum sponsored by Robert Appel, Vermont's defender general. The topic was the death penalty. The speakers, in addition to Mr. Appel, were Russell Neufeld, a capital defender from the Legal Aid Society of New York City, and Shujaa Graham, a man from California who was convicted of murder and sentenced to death, but whose conviction was overturned and who was eventually acquitted of the crime, evidently because the jurors in his fourth trial became convinced he had been framed by the California authorities.

All these men are intimately acquainted with the details of violent crime in America, and they all testified persuasively, based on the crimes they have encountered, that the risk of being killed by the state has no deterrent effect whatsoever on people who commit violent crimes. Most of the time, violent crimes are done under conditions that offer no opportunity to think about what's going to come later, and they tend to be done by people in either an intellectual or an emotional state that doesn't permit thinking of the future. The testimony last night confirmed many writings I have seen previously which offer ample evidence that the deterrent effect of the death penalty doesn't exist. Even so, the majority of the American people, including most notable politicians, continue to support the hideous practice of using the state governments and the nation to kill helpless people in their custody. More often than not the reason given is the deterrent effect of the penalty.

How can this be, we ask? How can it be in a world where every other country with a heritage and educational level similar to ours has abolished it? How can it be when our closest block of allies, the European Union, has made the absence of the death penalty a requirement for membership? How can it be when our continuing on with the miserable business makes us, as a nation, foul in the eyes of the people whose respect we most desire?

Jacques Barzun has given us the answer: reason working on fragments of experience. We know that if we stick our hand on a hot stove the result deters us from doing it again. When we see it happen to someone else, we become more careful. From this fragment of experience people who can't imagine complexity reason that the same process must work with respect to killing people. We know that certain acts can lead to being strapped on a gurney and having poison injected into the veins, and so we are deterred from those acts. People who think in this way have the ability to blot out a million differences in order to concentrate on a single similarity. And, low and behold: that one similarity is what allows them to do as they want.

I realize that other reasons besides deterrence have been put forward in support of killing by the state. But after all the fancy language has been worked through, they all sugar down to revenge. It's a desire I can understand and respect to some extent. But it takes only the simplest analysis to see that revenge is not a business in which governments should engage.

Without the argument of deterrence, justification for the death penalty collapses. And belief in deterrence persists only through simple-mindedness.

This is only one of the more dramatic instances in which refusal to face the complexity of situation leads to bad thinking. If one wanted to begin detailing them, he could fill libraries and scarcely be started. You would think that the university world is a realm where the simplistic rush to conclusion would be resisted. It probably would be if education held the place in the university that it should. But education is far below the top of university concerns and slips farther down each time the degree salesmen tighten their grip.

This might be a good place to interject that I'm not a purist with respect to universities. They are clearly places for training, for social manipulation, for boosting economic growth, for maintaining a system of social snobbery perhaps less vicious than other systems have been, and for providing employment to a class of people who, without them, would be forced onto public welfare. These are all laudable activities which humanity, in its present state, can't do without. I wouldn't even want the university to become pure. Purity is a quality that generally gives me the willies. But, I would like for education to have a place in the university, and a place near its heart.

If education were more central and did provide a foundation for university life, the practice of respecting complexity would probably modify university behavior more than any other single thing. You'll recall that I said in the seventh letter of this series that it's an iffy question whether the university sponsors more activities that are educational than are miseducational. If we wanted to reduce the latter, the most effective thing we could do would be to scrutinize all the established disciplines with respect to how intelligently they address the complexities that presumably fall within their jurisdiction. A formidable series of books could be written, doing this discipline by discipline. I wish someone would take on the task, but, alas, it won't be me. The best I can do is make a few suggestions to indicate how the effort might proceed.

We could begin with the most notorious discipline in the university, the one misnamed "Education," which is actually devoted to the process of rationing teaching certificates to college graduates. It's supposed to teach people how to teach, but it has allowed that art to be run over by an abstractionism gone mad based on the notion that children are natural rather than social constructs (or ,God forbid, creations of Providence). As we all know, natural products are produced in stages—a stalk of corn three weeks out of the ground is a different thing from a stalk of corn ten weeks old in August—so if we want to deal with them, we've got to know what stage they're in. And, laying out the stages children are in is mainly what the "Educational" discipline is about. I'll grant that educationists pay lip service to the notion that each child is influenced by social factors (for historical factors they don't even bother with lip service), but that has very little effect on what they instruct prospective teachers to do. The American public remains largely unaware of the degree to which a simplistic developmentalism dominates the schools or of the various ways it operates to vitiate teaching. But the public does know something is seriously wrong, and that's why we now have waves of political flappy-doodle about vouchers and so forth.

I can't argue that a simplistic naturalism is the only reason public schools are less enriching than they ought to be. Other factors are at work, including the age-old factor of dull-brained vested interest. Yet, I do believe that if teachers were not only free, but encouraged, to see children as social and historical creatures, we would open a flood of teaching energy and imagination that would go a long way towards refurbishing institutions that once were the pride of American life. To do it, though, would require that teachers become educated persons and not just trainees in developmentalism.

What need has a third-grade teacher, people are always asking, to know anything about the Thirty Years War or the writings of Aristotle? She doesn't teach the kids about those things. The question reveals the thought behind it. In this view, the teacher is not an experienced human being interacting with those less experienced to suggest to them how life can be well-lived. Rather, she is a functionary, managing stages. And there's no reason for a functionary to model educated speech and behavior, not as long as she functions in the prescribed mode.

A great cry has gone up throughout the nation that the students no longer respect the teachers. My question is, if the teachers behave as they are told to by the professional educators, why should the students respect them?

One more example of how refusal to confront complexity cripples thought, and then I'll be done for today. This one's from the so-called social science of economics.

As everyone knows, economists compile a quarterly figure known as the GDP or gross domestic product. According to a leading economic text, "Gross domestic product or GDP is the broadest measure of the health of the US economy." Politicians rant about it. Elections turn on it. People take credit for it when it goes up and try to escape responsibility for it when it goes down. It's a very big deal. But scarcely anyone bothers to ask how the number is put together or whether it really is a measure of the "health" of the economy of the nation. In fact, in the view of economists, and of the politicians who take them as gurus, the GDP defines economic health, rather than being simply one measure of it.

You remember how when we were in grammar school our teachers told us we couldn't add apples and oranges and get a number that made any sense? The GDP involves exactly that kind of addition. Completely unlike things are added together as though they were reinforcing one another to reach a substance greater than either. If a farmer grows a field of wheat and sells it for $50,000, that amount is added to the GDP. If the next week a tornado comes along and destroys the farmer's house, and he has to pay $50,000 just to put it back as it was, that payment is also added to the GDP. From the farmer's point of view, and from the point of view of logic, the poor guy has, at best, broken even, and lost his labor in the process. From the reasoning of the GDP, the nation's wealth has increased by $100,000. If we want really to get rich, I guess we need a nuclear attack.

Why is this sort of thing tolerated? You know as well as I. People want easy answers. They want a number they can parrot to say that things are either okay or terrible. They want to be able to base their actions on a simple indicator rather than having to think. And, it takes only a very little thought to recognize that relying on single indicators to describe a complex phenomenon like the economic health of a nation is idiotic. At any given time, some people are getting rich, and some are suffering terrible embarrassments and discomfort. An educated people would not allow artificially concocted, simplistic numbers to divert them from addressing the disorders that are right in their faces, crying for attention. But, all too often, that's the effect of the social sciences.

Virtually all of social science is based on ignoring variables that control outcomes. Yet, in some form or other, social science is the primary activity of American universities today. That shows clearly where education stands. In a university that put education first, students would always be asked to investigate how the answers their disciplines offer relate to the complexity the disciplines profess to illuminate. In our teaching and learning, that rarely happens.

I have one more great refusal, and I'll go on to it next time.

*There are many conditions within the university community
which are hard to imagine from outside. Here I take up one that
may cause more harm than any other: the unwillingness to ask
seriously why we study what we do.*

*T*HE THIRD OF the great refusals lies at the heart of the curriculum
commotion which has agitated higher education over the past twenty-five
years. As you know, defenders of tradition have decried the withering of
classical studies because without them we lose cultural continuity. By contrast, proponents of liberal change have said that cultural continuity is the
problem in education because it continues to exclude minorities and women,
and consequently that the canon should be deconstructed, in all the senses
of that benighted term. Both these arguments are silly, though in this
one case I have to admit that those on the left are even sillier than those on
the right.

The confusion arises because neither side of the debate will inquire seriously into the question of why certain texts should be chosen as material
for study in schools and colleges. The standard of selection is the issue the
modern academy, twitterpated by the timidity of the degree salesmen, re-
fuses to face. Modern educators need to be reminded of the argument of
one of your favorites, Montaigne (who, incidentally, has almost dropped
out of the curriculum of higher education), that the goal of education is a
mind well made, not a mind well filled.

What is it that makes for strong, imaginative, curious, and critical minds?
That's the question for education, not what will boost somebody's pet ideology. Once we address the curricular riddle that way, finding solutions

becomes possible. But so long as people are trying to solve it by pushing political and economic agendas there is no way out of the tangle, and the universities will continue trying to turn out benign, malleable automatons rather than thinking men and women.

A principal disgrace of the modern university is that students are not only permitted, they are encouraged, to waste their time, energy, and money on flaccid texts that do nothing for their agility of mind. They speak and write badly because they read badly. I think they have the right to be guided towards materials that will make them stronger, and away from materials that will tend to turn them into parrots. And, obviously, some teachers do this. They are the intellectual heroes of the academy, but they aren't in the majority.

A charge regularly lodged against those who support the reading of books that have been around for a while is that they are elitists. Why it's more elite to read Shakespeare than a text by an addled business school professor writing on total quality management is beyond my understanding. The implication is that only a small percentage of students can read Shakespeare profitably. This is not only a lie; it's a goddamned lie put forward by those who know somewhere in the backs of their control-freak brains that if we did have a student population who were nourished by provocative works like the plays and poems of Shakespeare they would be less likely to march off into the slots that have been prepared for them, or, at least, less likely to see themselves as nothing more than pegs for those slots.

For years I've enjoyed the essays of Lewis Lapham, the editor of *Harper's Magazine*. But though he was fun to read, I used to think he was a bit over the top, exaggerated, a practitioner of sarcasm for its own sake. Lately, however, as I've tried more fully to open my own eyes, Lapham strikes me as getting closer to the truth. In his editorial titled "School Bells," which appeared in a recent issue, he says that Americans don't want their schools to get better because we wouldn't know what to do with an educated population, that politicians depend on an uninformed electorate for their safety in office, and that the marketers of the gross domestic product depend upon the eager and uncritical consumption of junk. He then goes on to comment, "The country's reserves of ignorance constitute a natural resource as precious as the Mississippi River or the long-lost herds of buffalo."

I'm not as ready to believe in conscious conspiracy theories as Lapham seems to be. The reasons for refusing to base university studies on sustaining literature are too numerous and complex for us ever to sort them out completely. They even include a tincture of idealism of the sort that is displayed by educators who think you can get lower-middle class boys to read by giving them stories about racing car drivers who spend their time drinking beer when they aren't out on the track—something relevant, you know. The effect, however, of this variety of refusal is as though it were a conspiracy to keep the proletariate obedient in their lockstep lives.

Perhaps the most formidable challenge in liberal arts teaching comes from the truth that people don't imagine the reward of good literature—I'm speaking of good literature in the sense of all fine writing—until they have experienced it. Furthermore, it's an experience that's usually not instantaneous. It has to rise before it can sweep one away. This means that getting to it demands a kind of faith in the testimony of previous generations.

I mentioned earlier that back in the days when I was teaching in Norwich's Adult Degree Program, I would occasionally offer a seminar on some portion of Shakespeare's writing. I did this expecting that the enrollees would generally be fans of Shakespeare, people who had read the plays previously and wanted to read them again alongside interesting companions.

That turned out not to be the case. Most of the people who signed up had read no Shakespeare at all. They came because he was a name they felt a vague obligation to explore. Weak as such impulses are, I thank Heaven for them.

Many of these students were not strong readers. They found the plays difficult at first, even bewildering. But we persevered. I would read passages aloud. We listened to a few tapes. We saw movies. Invariably the time came for all of them, usually during a quiet moment after we had discussed a scene, when they would look up with an almost startled expression, and exclaim something to the effect: "My God! He really is great!"

On these occasions the cynic in me would say, furtively, "Wow! No fooling!" But the cynic flashed and disappeared. What remained was the finest joy I had in teaching. Silly as it may sound to pronounce Shakespeare a great writer, it was for them a genuine, fresh acknowledgement. He was no longer just one of those imposing names. Right there on the page they saw it, and knew it: the power and beauty of the English language shaped and wielded as they had not known it could be. After that, everything about language was different.

A genuine encounter with Shakespeare is not just a matter of appreciating him. It brings out of students' minds ideas and attitudes that previously couldn't find release. I recall one day when we were talking about the second scene of the first act of *Richard III*, where Richard encounters Lady Anne, whose husband and father-in-law he has murdered, and immediately begins to woe her. The students were perplexed because there could scarcely be more villainous actions than Richard has done, and yet, they somehow found themselves pulling for him. They thrilled when he announced that Anne herself was the cause of the deaths, because of her appeal:

> Your beauty, that did haunt me in my sleep
> To undertake the death of all the world
> So might I live one hour in your sweet bosom.

"How can we like this guy?" somebody asked.

And then somebody else: "Maybe it's because he's so damned alive. Who else would have the guts to do anything like this?"

"And maybe being alive, in a way, is more important than being good, you know?" said another, hesitantly.

And, from a young lady who usually didn't talk much in the group: "Besides, who wouldn't be a little won over by a guy who would kill the whole world for you?"

We don't get thoughts like these from just any text. We don't get them unless the language has made improbable thoughts plausible. We don't get them from the latest maundering on market strategy.

"And why should we want them?" the degree salesmen will ask. And when they do, then the issue is really joined. The question of what we read is not just an idle matter of taste; it is not like deciding between chocolate and vanilla. It goes to the heart of who we want to be, and what sort of creatures we want to spend our lives among.

The truth is that many of our fellow citizens, and particularly those who see themselves as being in control, want other people to be exactly as dependable as machines are. When the right button is pushed, then the machine acts as we wish. It puts forth no surprises. To give the devil his due, we must admit that we all want that from other people sometimes. When we walk up to the ticket office and plop down our five, or six, or seven bucks, we want the person on the other side of the glass to issue us the ticket we've asked for and not to question why we've chosen to see this film rather than another. A goodly portion of our human interactions each day fall into this category. They may be accompanied by a smile, or an offhand remark, but the point is, we want what we want from the person we're confronting, and we expect to get it.

The question is not whether we want some of our interactions to be nearly automatic. Obviously, we do. But, do we want them all to be that way?

The answer we get increasingly from our social and institutional leaders is yes. They want life to be perfectly predictable, perfectly safe, perfectly habitual. Everybody gets up everyday and goes to his job, and comes back to his house, and pays the mortgage every month on the same day, and has his supper at the same time every night. This is the American way. This is the

American dream. As Jacques Barzun said, self-reliance in America was gradually replaced by its opposite. We don't need self reliance when systems take care of everything.

It sounds pretty good until we begin to consider the cost. If everybody else is going to be a machine to you, then you've got to be a machine to them. And incrementally, if you're a machine to everybody you encounter, you'll become a machine to yourself. At that point, the entire enterprise begins to be questionable. If everything is working automatically, and if no one is living a spontaneous life outside the automation, why should anything work at all? Why not just shut the whole business down?

Education is the activity by which we answer that question. And, in education, we thrive on uncertainty; we thrive on unexpected responses that require us, at times, to entertain surprising thoughts. If we want to have such thoughts, in order to lead spontaneous lives, the sort of lives that require mental and emotional agility, then we've got to be in touch with stimuli that will bring those thoughts out of us. This is why we read Shakespeare, and Montaigne, and Wordsworth, and Jane Austen, and Charles Dickens. They aren't for cultural continuity, nor for blueprinting the right ideological program. They are for well-made minds, that is, if you think a mind well-made is a mind that thinks rather than one that reacts predictably. The degree salesmen refuse to ask how to make good minds because they refuse to ask what a good mind is. And so, it comes naturally to them to refuse to inquire about the materials to aid that quest and, instead, gravitate towards materials that are supplied most readily by commercial enterprise. Among the great refusals, this may be the one that's most disgusting, though I think they're all about equal in their bad effects.

Next time, I'll turn towards the principal modes of learning and perceiving that are necessary for education. I'll send the first letter on that subject in a week or so.

Here I began the first of three discussions of the primary avenues to life which students in modern universities do not examine very carefully. I started with romanticism.

*B*ELIEVE IT OR not, I was once not only a candidate for the presidency of a small college but was one of three people recommended to the board of trustees by the search committee. The board interviewed me in a meeting room at Logan Airport and took nearly all of an afternoon to do it. Midway in the session somebody asked me what I thought was the most important thing for a student in college to learn, and I made the disastrous mistake of answering truthfully. From that moment I could feel the whole business going downhill. Afterwards, I never heard from the board about their decision, but once a couple months had passed I concluded I hadn't been selected.

What I said during my fit of truthfulness was that I thought every student needed to be introduced to the principal approaches to life and to begin to decide how his or her own existence was going to relate to them. Then I continued with the remark that though all the major modes were important, the romantic approach was the one with which undergraduate students should begin.

You know how it is when you say something in a room and can tell from the radical silence that you've struck bone? I never had the sensation more strongly than after mentioning the romantic mode. I might as well have been speaking Martian. I doubt it had occurred to any member of my audience that history lays out ways for people to respond to life's mysteries and offers examples of the grandeur and danger of each approach. Naive people believe they make up everything by themselves and in that respect are like puppets dancing on strings they have not bothered to look up and see.

To go through life deceived about your own autonomy, thinking you're in control when actually you've made no serious decisions, strikes me as pathetic business. Some might argue that if you can hold on to that level of self-deception all the way through, it's okay. In theory it might be, but it's similar to saying that it would have been better never to have entered existence at all. It's not a position a sentient being can seriously entertain. So, despite my downfall, I would repeat that students should learn to recognize the prizes and perils involved in moving in and out of the modes humanity has devised for making meaning of life. And I start with the romantic mode because traditionally it has been the most tempting to youth. After spending the rest of this letter on it, I'll go on in letters fourteen and fifteen to the classical and the modern modes.

Of all words in English, "romance" and "romantic" may have been the source of largest dispute. The eminent historian of ideas Arthur Lovejoy once wrote an essay in which he sketched so many definitions for "romanticism" that he said it had become deprived of any meaning at all. Yet, despite its myriad meanings, it's a word we can't do without. That's because it summarizes the sensibility that leads to the most intense and extensive pleasures.

In modern America we live in such a gradgrind world that the concept of pleasure has become linked to immorality. If somebody is having fun, then he must be doing something wrong: that's the conventional wisdom which the people who consider themselves in charge are trying to foist on the rest of us. It's as though they're pushing Honorius, of Childe Harold's tale, as our patron saint, he who lived "In hope to merit Heaven, by making earth a Hell." Study hard so you can grow up to buy houses and insurance policies, the young people are told. Then, there's great surprise that some of them revolt and even go so far as to smoke marijuana cigarettes and listen to jangly music.

What in Holy Hell is wrong with them? What's wrong is that the official world is trying to build a wall between them and all manifestations of romance. And they, in their despair, are trying to break through it, often in fairly stupid ways. And what is this romance that they're so desperate to attain? It's not hard to find descriptions of it. There's a pretty good summary in the book by Barzun we've been discussing. It's the notion that thought and feeling should support one another, and not be at war. That exploring and discovering are worth taking some risks for. That religion resides not so much in institutions and doctrines, but in our own hearts. That spirit is a reality which can be approached through nature and art. That each of us has an inner knowledge on which he must act if he is to find a meaning in life. That the truth lies in particulars, in what we see and feel right in front of us, and not in the abstractions that are preached from pulpits, and CEO offices, and the lairs of the degree salesmen. That we are linked by invisible bonds to the past, which can never be broken, and which must be honored in the present. That greatness can rise out of ordinary life and does not always have to be ordained and credentialed. That love imbues life's purpose and that without it the rest is trash.

These are legitimate propositions, and though there's danger in them, as there is in anything of worth, to dismiss them in order to avoid the danger is the approach of weak and craven minds. Young people know this, and when they confront a so-called educational system that doesn't take romance seriously, and that doesn't attempt to teach them its ins and outs, they are right to reject it.

The extent to which they do reject current teaching is acknowledged by almost no one in the university world, and certainly not by the degree salesmen with their glossy-paged publications peppered with phony scenes of student eagerness. If you want a more honest picture, walk up and down the halls of a middling American university during class time, peer into the rooms and observe the students' faces. You'll seldom find eagerness there. What you see instead is a population of young people marking time in order to get their tickets punched. Some of them may be trying not to go to sleep. But many don't make even that effort.

When we acknowledge the necessity of the romantic mode, we are still left with the question of how to teach it. The answers aren't self-evident, but they are more approachable once we understand that the materials selected are being engaged for the sake of helping students decide how romance should figure in their own lives. Any number of techniques might work, but for myself I have nothing against the obvious. It is too often rejected for that reason alone.

We have, after all, in our own cultural history a time known as the Romantic Era, in which powerful writers and thinkers explored the romantic propositions. They are certainly not the only persons to have done so. We can find romantic sensibilities sprinkled throughout human history. Still, I see nothing wrong in starting with Wordsworth and Coleridge, Keats and Shelley, Scott and Longfellow, Emerson and Thoreau, Poe and Whittier, Eliot and Dickens. A college curriculum that knows nothing of any of them is surely a dubious enterprise.

With respect to what was once a tradition, by the way, the people of our grandparents' generation had a wisdom we have lost and ought to try to recover. They knew and repeated near-mythic tales, often grounded in an element of history, which presented to school children noble deeds and romantic heroes. Lately we have prided ourselves on becoming too sophisticated for these. We know that the past was not as these stories paint it. We have taken off the rose-colored glasses; we see things straight on in their grimy detail. There's some good in our practice, but it can be pushed beyond reason and produce its own distortions. Shelley, in his essay "A Defense of Poetry," which is itself one of the grand works of romantic sensibility, says that when we reject products of social imagination and practice an "unmitigated exercise of the calculating faculty" it always creates a social fissure, with the rich growing richer on one side and the poor poorer on the other. It brings us closer either to anarchy or despotism. I wouldn't want the current Republican presidential candidate to charge me with promoting class warfare, but it seems to me that we are, indeed, closer to both those conditions in America than we once were and that the cause is related to the extraction of romance from public life.

Whittier's ballad of Barbara Frietchie, for example, is neither philosophically deep nor rhetorically complex, and may not even tell a "true" story, but I continue to think it's a wonderful piece of American literature, which speaks powerfully to ideals and can be read with pleasure by any grade-school child. I still, today, even in my jaded old age, get a thrill from its opening:

> Up from the meadows rich with corn,
> Clear in the cool September morn,
> The clustered spires of Frederick stand
> Green-walled by the hills of Maryland.

The words that come at the climatic moment, when Stonewall Jackson's soldiers are about to obliterate the banner waving from Barbara Frietchie's house—

> She leaned far out on the window sill
> And shook it forth with a royal will.
> "Shoot if you must this old grey head,
> But spare your country's flag," she said—

are worth turning over in our minds to ask whether the heroism they convey still has value in it, and whether it can find modern opportunities. If we have got too fancy to pay attention to words like these then we may have got too fancy for life.

Another point Shelley makes in his essay on poetry is that corruption in any system has as its purpose the destruction of all true pleasure, especially pleasure that is deepest and most long-lasting. "It begins at the imagination and the intellect as at the core and distributes itself thence as a paralyzing venom." This is a reasonably apt description of what the degree salesmen have been doing in the colleges and universities. The studies with the potential to produce the most intense pleasure are increasingly discounted and shoved aside in favor of those the degree salesmen think they can sell more readily to a calculating world. There are more students in universities today concentrating on forms of management and administration than on literature, history, and philosophy all together. And, guess what? People aren't studying these so-called practical subjects for the pleasure in them. There is no pleasure in them. What's being sought is a dollar return on investment with as little personal transformation as possible.

Shelley's right. The only potent counters to corruption and, ultimately, to pure evil are the agencies of romance: love, beauty, poetry in all its forms, historical revery, a sense of spirit that transcends the self. That each of these quests can be misused, and can lead people astray, doesn't alter the truth that without them there's no place to go except straight into the pit. If there are qualities of life that have to be understood and engaged in order to give life any sense at all, why should they not be examined in university studies? What can we study that is more important? Anybody who advises against them you have to figure is either deluded or engaged in some sort of racket.

I could be partial to romanticism because bringing it up twenty years ago may have saved me from a terrible fate. God knows what would have happened if I had become a college president. I can't imagine it would have been good. But whether or not I'm right to put romanticism first on my list of fundamental stances, I have no doubt it belongs in the lessons every college student should take up. If we don't know our relation to the values romanticism has put forward, we don't know much about ourselves at all.

Next time I'll go on to an approach that may appeal more than romanticism does to the sober side of our nature. You can look for it in about a week.

The second approach to life, in this section of three, has become associated with the period we call the classical age. It may be inaccurate to call it that because we mean to designate by the term the finest, highest, and most honorable behavior humans have exhibited and there's scant evidence that the people who lived a long time ago are any better than we are. Still, their literature emphasized qualities which modern literature, fearful of sentimentality, has shied away from.

*I*N THE PREFACE to the second edition of *Lyrical Ballads*, Wordsworth argues that one person is elevated over another by the intensity of feeling he possesses. This is, indeed, the watchword of the romantic movement, which places a high valuation on passion and the risk that seems inevitably to run alongside it. There's a good deal to be said for the concept. Perhaps it's self-evident that sluggish feelings produce fundamental human lowness which no amount of management or routine can overcome. They are surely a source of corruption in the modern university, where they are now practiced consummately by those in charge. No one capable of deep feeling would put dollars above education in the regular manner of our officialdom, though in the case of the degree salesmen this is a willed innocence of understanding and consequently not one deserving major reserves of sympathy

I don't think, however, that the elevating power of strong feeling provides the entire meaning of human endeavor. Though intensity is an elemental quality in humans, the intelligent management of intensity is probably just as important. It was the latter which drew the prime attention of the period we've come to call the classical age, and the contribution it made to human thought continues to be so vital that no serious educational process can ignore it.

As with Romanticism, the classical temper can be studied in many ways using a vast range of materials. Fundamental approaches to life permeate all human history. My own lessons in this mode, however, have come from common sources, and I don't think they're any the worse for it. Plutarch is a good place to begin because he remains, as Mme. Roland said, "the pasturage of great souls," and because he was till recently the possession of all people in the West who wished to educate themselves. Over the past few weeks I've been reading the translation of the *Lives* by Ian Scott-Kilvert and comparing them with the traditional Dryden translation. I think in this case the later version is superior because I suspect it comes closer to the straightforward style of the original. I can think of no one who simply wanted to get the story told more than Plutarch did.

His life of Fabius Maximus serves as a primer on classical virtue because Fabius, throughout his public career, was unable to achieve a final and secure victory and was required instead to hold on to what was possible when winning was out of reach. He was confronted by Hannibal, one of the great commanders of history, and certainly the strongest foe the Romans had ever faced. Fabius believed that since any direct clash was likely to lead to defeat the best policy was to wear Hannibal down. So he remained always in a defensive posture, enduring the taunts of his rivals that he was timid to the point of cowardice. During one of his periods out of power, however, his successor Terentius Varro, who had bragged that he would smash Hannibal within a day after he was given command, was lured into battle at Cannae, and for his day's work, rather than vanquishing the Carthaginians, lost fifty thousand Roman lives and put the capital city in danger. The people who had been scorning Fabius turned to him in panic and asked that he organize the defenses of Rome, which he did calmly and with superior competence. His story teaches that there is always something to be done, even when things aren't going well, and that if you'll keep your head and summon your courage, you'll be better off than to let panic take over. Yet we have to proceed in this faith knowing there are no guarantees, because absurd conditions and absurd men are always present. We may wish to reduce the supply of the latter, but as far as I can tell they have as great a staying power as roaches.

The reason we can count on the presence of absurd people is that they feed off an enduring weakness, the desire to shine in other people's eyes, regardless of who those people are. We see this spelled out clearly in Plutarch, over and again. Varro, for example, sought the defeat of Hannibal for his own glory. The good of Rome was a secondary consideration. Consequently, he violated a principal rule of classical virtue, that one should not gamble with other people's well-being in the hope of winning something for oneself. Few, and perhaps no, men are consciously evil, but a great many fall to evil-doing because they wish to use other people as commodities in their own campaigns for prestige. Wanting to strut on the stage clouds judgment more than anything else and in the absence of classical restraint leads to nonsense and disaster.

If the purpose of romanticism is to enable us to enhance pleasure, the purpose of classicism is to help us endure absurdity. Since the world is divided between the two, we need both modes—I suspect in about equal measure—to live educated lives. They should be seen not as alternatives but as complements to one another.

Another way of distinguishing the two is to put the prime question to both life and death: what is each for? Life is for the sweetness thereof, and death is for teaching us how and why to give it up. Paul Fussell, in his autobiography *Doing Battle* (which, by the way, is a fine book), in paying tribute to H. L. Mencken, says that despite his acute insights Mencken exhibited an intellectual weakness common among his countrymen: "He didn't respond to the classical understanding that all human life is destined to failure, and that only tragic irony is capable of offering a grown up vision."

Fussell is right in a certain respect. Each day can be seen as a step towards death, and if we think of death as failure, which it is in a way, then an ironic perspective is required to endure it. Though I'm drawn to Fussell's open-eyed courage, derived from his having seen numerous lives destroyed by the insanities of war, it strikes me that by itself it may be overly bleak. It should be tempered by the kind of lengthy perspective I mentioned in letter number nine. By bringing the long view into account we stumble across an interesting merger of the romantic and classical approaches.

A good source for studying this amalgam is Tennyson's poem "Tiresias," which relates the legend of the blind poet's encounter with Meneceus, a descendant of Cadmus, who had brought the curse of the sphinx down on his city of Thebes. The only way the monster can be placated is by the sacrifice of someone from Cadmus's line, and when Tiresias tells the boy this hard truth he also reminds him that:

> No sound is breathed so potent to coerce
> And to conciliate, as their names who dare
> For that sweet motherland which gave them birth
> Nobly to do, nobly to die. Their names
> Graven on memorial columns, are a song
> Heard in the future; few, but more than wall
> And rampart, their examples reach a hand
> Far through all years, and everywhere they meet
> And kindle generous purpose, and the strength
> To mould it into action pure as theirs.

Years ago, when I was living in Maryland, I memorized this poem, which is fairly long (177 lines), as a kind of mental exercise. As I would chant it aloud to myself during afternoon walks along the Potomac, my mind would linger on this passage and reflect that the sentiment behind it has been mixed with so much fraudulent rhetoric from pompous politicians and generals its power has been largely negated. Yet, it's a mistake to let self-serving dimwits usurp worthy principles. If situations do arise in which great sacrifice could kindle generous purpose in the future, then sacrifice may be justified. That, at least, is the classical proposition. It's worth reminding ourselves of from time to time, though we should also keep in mind that when folks are asking us for sacrifices they're not willing to make themselves, we would do well to be wary.

Though communal sacrifice is a potent feature of the classical ethic, it has to stand down in favor of the one I'll conclude with today: holding out to the end, even in the face of certain defeat. Setting this as the groundwork of the classical mode confirms the reign of irony in human sensibility. Here at the heart of the system we've thought of as most charged with logic is a principle that appears to have no logic at all. When I was a young soldier, the first sergeant of my training company was an imposing man in his forties who had been a member of the ranger regiment that landed at Salerno and fought all the way up the Italian peninsula. He told us that as soon as he and his comrades got into contact with the enemy they let the Germans know they didn't expect to be taken prisoner and that they didn't intend to take any prisoners themselves. Then he exclaimed that this was the same spirit under which our training exercises would be conducted. I can remember thinking simultaneously that I admired him immensely and that he was a maniac. Today, I would probably lean more toward the latter than the former judgment. Yet, he sticks in my mind as a curious symbol of something that's easy to forget in this squishy era: there are times when compromise is not called for. It is not our job to find the middle ground between God and the Devil.

We should, of course, be very careful when we get it into our heads that we're on God's side. Those times don't come often, and if we think we've blundered into one we ought to consider—and consider deeply— the possibility of our own pigheadedness. Yet, they do come, and education should incorporate lessons in how to handle them.

There's a poem from the 1850s I've grown increasingly fond of over the years even though it's one I don't think I've ever heard mentioned in my circle of acquaintances. I first read Robert Browning's "Childe Roland to the Dark Tower Came" when I was studying with Edgar Shannon at the University of Virginia. For that reason, perhaps, the poem and the man are fused in my mind and stand for a quality I've never been able to describe adequately but which, when I'm forced to a crude approximation, presents itself as a fabric of sensibility draping a frame of steel.

The poem, in wonderfully surreal, nightmarish language, tells of a pilgrim who deserts the beaten course, directed on the new way by a "hoary cripple with malicious eye" who clearly intends to lead him to disaster. He sets out through a hellish landscape that hides the Dark Tower, seeking it with no hope that it will bring him any kind of ordinary reward. The body of the poem describes the journey through a realm so bad nothing can cure it other than "the Last Judgment's fire." The grass there is like leper's hair. The only living thing he sees is a "stiff blind horse, his every bone a-stare" kicked out of the devil's stud. In other words, the entire world has become hideous, and there's nothing to be done except keep on. As he comes near to the final place, "the round squat turret blind as the fool's heart," he realizes he is being watched by the spirits of all those who had gone before him, and been brave, and suffered defeat, and now are ranging the hillsides:

> To view the last of me, a living frame
> For one more picture!

One more picture of human desolation in the offing, and then we have the final lines of the poem:
> I saw them and I knew them all. And yet
> Dauntless the slug-horn to my lips I set,
>   And blew. *"Childe Roland to the Dark Tower came."*

Most of Browning's acquaintances were mystified by the piece, but when one of his friends asked him whether its meaning could be expressed as "He that endureth to the end shall be saved," Browning answered, "Yes, just about that."

And, so he shall be saved, but not in the way children imagine: that's the core message of the classical mode.

Neither the romantic nor the classical vision is much in vogue right now. Next time I'll talk about what we're trying to set in their place.

A third mode of life, which increasingly rules the land, has mostly escaped examination—by the university or anybody else— because it passes as what must be. It is that which is done, that which must be obeyed, because not to do it or obey it would be unthinkable to right-thinking people.

*I*N THIS FIFTEENTH letter I'll try to define a third mode of dealing with life that has coalesced so recently you can't find much written about it but that has attained such power no education which fails to attend to it can be adequate. It has no accepted name. I've come to think of it as modern prudence, though the term "modern" has connotations that don't fit with it perfectly. I hope by the time I get to the end I can say enough about it to show how the "modernism" of common definition has spawned a prudence that turns back on itself.

To understand the centrality the latter has attained we need to recall Tocqueville's warning that people don't generally care much about a goal until they get close to it, but when the substance of it has been achieved they then drive themselves nuts trying to bring it to perfection. He made the point with respect to social equality, noting that Americans, who pretty much had it, were a lot more worried about it than the Europeans, for whom it was still a long way off. The same truth pertains to most conditions people think they want, and it certainly holds with biological and social security, which is the concern I'm taking up today.

If we were to take seriously the current teaching about safety beamed at us from all the media, we would have to conclude that my survival past the age of twelve was a miracle. When I rode my bicycle I didn't wear a helmet;

when I rode in the car, I didn't sit in the back seat with my safety belt fastened; when I sailed in a boat, I didn't have a life preserver. No one ever checked me for the seven signs of cancer. When I went out to play after school, my mother didn't know where I was and could not have found me if she had searched. She certainly didn't know that my friend Richard Osborn and I were often swimming across the river and throwing oyster shells at the alligators that sunned themselves on the opposite bank, nor did she know that we regularly played a game called "chicken" where we paced off twenty-five yards between us and stood and fired our B-B guns at one another until one of us felt the sting a bit too much and laid his gun down. She didn't know that, in quest of bats, which Richard's brother Walter said he would pay us a quarter a piece for, we dived into the river just past the Hillsborough Avenue Bridge and swam up the sewer pipe till we got out of the water and then trekked four miles underground until we climbed out of a manhole on Central Avenue with two bats in our bag, which Walter (the cheap jerk) refused to pay us for because he said they were too little. I lived, in short, a perfectly normal boy's life.

I suspect boys nowadays do similar things. The difference now is that they have to break rules to do them, whereas, as far as I know, Richard and I broke no rules at all. We didn't break any because there weren't any. Nobody was making regulations to insure our safety. The adult world didn't care what we did as long as we showed up for supper. Was this neglect? I didn't think so. It always seemed to me that my mother loved me.

I'm not telling these stories to make an invidious comparison. The past can't be resurrected nor, probably, should it be. It had its own problems. I want simply to point out that now we are far more intensely regulated than we were just a short while ago and the change has been so radical as to have transformed the temper and feel of life.

Nearly all the regulations that have been enacted over the past generation have been put forward in the interests of safety and security. An alteration of this scope raises the question of why safety suddenly vaulted out of the pack—stopped being one of many—and became the dominant issue of social life. Things like this don't happen accidentally. They are caused. Though we can't follow the train of causation perfectly, we can discover associations and logical consequences that help us understand the makeup of a situation better than when we take it for granted. Taking a thing for granted means that it functions as a trap, whereas if we know what makes it tick we have a chance of getting out of it if we decide we want to.

Whether or not the end of this millennium means the end of something real, it's hard to deny that the intellectual and artistic efforts of the twentieth century constituted an adversarial culture. It was concentrated far more on tearing down than on building up. And, it was strikingly successful. Most of what stood as glorious, gorgeous, and inspiring in 1900 came under attack shortly afterwards. As Lionel Trilling put it, the destruction of the "specious good" became the principal goal of those who saw themselves as doing something culturally momentous.

Even after all recent gyrations of deconstruction and feminist attacks on the patriarchy are taken into account—and some of them have been fairly catchy—the most powerful document of the great demolition, in English, remains T. S. Eliot's *The Waste Land*. The irony of its power is that it depends on aesthetic standards which rise from the old culture now gone rancid, a beautiful poem advanced to unveil the ugliness of the decaying world. Those who have listened often to its rhythms have favorite passages that come perpetually to mind. I, for example, find myself continually recalling the scene where a callow bureaucrat arrives at his girlfriend's room for a sordid sexual encounter:

> He, the young man carbuncular, arrives,
> A small house agent's clerk, with one bold stare,
> One of the low on whom assurance sits
> As a silk hat on a Bradford millionaire.
> The time is now propitious, as he guesses,
> The meal is ended, she is bored and tired,
> Endeavors to engage her in caresses
> Which still are unreproved, if undesired.

Flushed and decided, he assaults at once;
Exploring hands encounter no defence;
His vanity requires no response
And makes a welcome of indifference.

It's a parable that reminds one of a degree salesman seeking a Ph. D., so he can get his foot in your door: pretending to be after one thing when he's really after another.

People in this condition are so close to being dead they might as well already have crossed over, which seems to be the point of my second-most favorite section, where the poet is musing on the "unreal city":

Under the brown fog of a winter dawn,
A crowd flowed over London Bridge, so many,
I had not thought death had undone so many.
Sighs, short and infrequent, were exhaled,
And each man fixed his eyes before his feet.
Flowed up the hill and down King William Street,
To where St. Mary Woolnoth kept the hours
With a dead sound on the final stroke of nine.
There I saw one I knew, and stopped him, crying "Stetson!
"You who were with me in the ships at Mylae!
"That corpse you planted last year in your garden,
"Has it begun to sprout? Will it bloom this year?

We have got to the situation where the only hint of brightness comes from the hope that something might spring out of putrefaction. What are people to do when they get to this stage?

In my newspaper this morning, Jeff Danziger has a cartoon showing old people playing cards at a resort in Miami. They're out of sorts over the cost of prescription drugs. One of them says, "We built this country. We want free pills." To which another rejoins, "I vote for anyone who gives me free pills." It would be hard to find a more perfect depiction of the modern sense of morality in action.

People want their pills and they want them as their right.

I've got nothing against free pills, but I do think it's worth asking why they have become the pre-eminent issue of our time. What are these pills that everyone has to have? It's clear that they have established themselves as the guardians of our well-being, and well-being is now defined as security and comfort. If all the former goods—honor, loyalty, love, victory over evil— have now been exposed as empty delusions, corpses to be planted in the garden, the corrupt symbols of a wasted land, then what is there to care about other than safety and comfort?

It's not an idle question. Maybe there is nothing else. Yet, whenever something sets itself up as the overweening good, education is required to put questions to it. The first question that comes to mind when somebody's trying to sell you something is, what does it cost?

The answer is everywhere. Yet, the majority remain blind to it. Turn to the page after the Danziger cartoon in my newspaper and you'll find an article with the headline: "Surveillance Becoming Standard in Britain." It's about the British attempt to reduce crime by putting cameras everywhere in the country, and it makes the point that when cameras scan all actions, not only criminal actions are recorded. For this advance towards public safety, the people pay with their privacy.

There's a comparable price for virtually all the provisions of modern prudence. The old folks who want their pills for free need to reflect that even if they can avoid plopping down their dollars, they still have to plop themselves down, for inspection by authority, before they can get their pills, or, at least, before they can get the really good ones.

Our old friend Jacques Barzun describes the cost of this blanket of safety as "the permanent spirit of inquisition." The most powerful theorist of the modern inquisition has been the French philosopher Michel Foucault, who, because of his clotted style, hasn't received the attention his analysis deserves. Foucault's principal thesis points towards the replacement of overt forms of power (the king's threat to cut your head off) with devious and discreet forms, exercised presumably for the purposes of beneficence. The practice of this modern form of power requires a vast network of authority which generally goes under the heading of professionalism. As it tightens its grip on human life, fewer and fewer activities are allowed to escape its notice. It's a form that has to be partly secret, partly hidden, in order to function, and it accomplishes this secrecy by masking itself as knowledge. In Foucault's analysis, professionalized knowledge and power are exactly the same thing, or, as he puts it in his inimitable style: "Between techniques of knowledge and strategies of power there is no exteriority."

It may be that the quest for safety under the guidance of those who have earned degrees in knowing what's good for people is the best humanity has to offer. Besides, it's not for education to say what mode of life one should adopt, but only to put questions to all the modes so they reveal themselves fully. I confess, though, for all the blessings of modern prudence, I now and then encounter features that give me pause. I read recently a news story from Italy where they have a law requiring motorbike riders to wear safety helmets. The police there were trying to give a ticket to a young man for not wearing a helmet. He wanted to avoid the ticket and tried to run away. So, they killed him. As I read the story I had the thought: maybe there's something to this Foucault after all. And could it be more than just silly nostalgia, a fondness for that boy swimming in the river, flirting with the alligators, breaking what would probably now be a dozen rules? I don't know. These things are hard to figure out.

On to another subject next time—the ethics of education.

The three letters beginning here address the ethics we have the right to expect from teachers. There has been much discussion lately of professional ethics, but most of it I've seen deals with promulgating milk-toast interactions to insure that no one's self-esteem is diminished. By ethics, I have something else in mind.

*I*T PROBABLY MAKES sense, now and then, to remind ourselves of where we are in this extravaganza. In the seventh letter, I said I was going to begin discussing the specific qualities of education. I started with three desirable habits, went on to how we might counter a set of refusals that hinder learning, then laid out three modes of approaching meaningful life that need to be included in any educational program. Now, in the final set of specifics, I'll have a go at some fundamental ethical practices demanded by the educated pursuit. The latter will take me through Letter 18, and then we'll be midway in the series. As my mother used to say, half done is well begun.

I can't claim that these twelve attributes make up a comprehensive list. Inventories of this sort can be extended endlessly. I do think though that if an educational program paid careful attention to even this dozen, simple as they are, it would be superior to most of those offered by current colleges and universities.

Educational ethics are violated by the professoriate more radically than are any other principles of good learning. This is because many professors live in intellectual ghettoes of their own designing and can't genuinely imagine that there are hopes, dreams, aspirations, concerns, and beliefs that transcend the issues of their small worlds. They do, of course, in a mode of fake ironic humor, make jokes about how nobody cares what they do, but this doesn't alter their conviction that what they do constitutes the only significant portion of the universe. I don't think it's possible to exaggerate the degree to which the average academic person, in pursuit of advancement, blinds himself to anything other than what will promote his career. And this, by the way, is what makes professors so highly manipulable by the degree salesmen.

It's a charge that can probably be brought against any set of ambitious people. It may even be seen as the way of the world and dismissed for that reason. There is, though, the difference that in professions outside education ethical behavior tends to be separable from moral stance. A physician might be a narrow-minded, arrogant, ambitious lout and still take your appendix out right. An attorney can be personally reprehensible and still win your case for you. We all know that businessmen are a long way from what we would wish but, still, they bring us interesting products. Moral obtuseness with them, though it may diminish their functioning, doesn't negate it. When we get to professors, however, it's a different deal. With them blindness to the moral demands of their calling not only takes away much of the good they might do, it can transform them into despoilers of minds. I know of no other profession—with the possible exception of politics—where getting on in it leads as generally to malfunction.

I should at this point make clear that I'm not saying that professors are immoral in a commonplace way. They are, for the most part, a kindly set, in the flaccid sense of that term. They would not kick a dog or take candy from a child. And though they are astoundingly cheap, most would not even cheat you out of a dollar. Few of them are bad people, but many are educationally unethical.

We can distinguish the two conditions by their sources. Outright immorality emerges from malice or selfishness, whereas ethical misbehavior is more often than not the result of thoughtlessness. The sad truth is that few professors think as hard as they should about what they are supposed to be doing. They take money from their students but they don't ask themselves hard questions about what their students are getting in return. Their neglect is made palatable for them by methodological self-deceptions which I'll spell out in the remainder of this letter and the two that follow.

Of all the temptations professors fall prey to, the most insidious is the notion that teaching and proselytizing are the same thing. The desire to win students over to some social, political, or religious position has ruined more teachers than anything else I've observed during my time in higher education. It has been rampant in the program I taught in until recently and, more than anything else, has held the program back from reaching its potential. The reason it's so powerful is that most professors do not have a genuine educational ideal that can temper and balance the social and political goals that have won their loyalty.

There's nothing wrong, of course, with professors having social and political loyalties. They would be brain-dead if they didn't. Nor is there anything wrong with letting students know what professors support. A teacher would have to put himself through ridiculous circumlocutions to avoid revealing what he thought about the issues of the day. But when the teacher comes to teach, personal loyalties should be set aside in the interest of helping the student understand fully and honestly the spectrum of opinion operating on the issue being examined. The positions the teacher dislikes have to be explored as openly and completely as those he treasures.

Some will say this is impossible. They are wrong. I know they're wrong because I have had students scream at me in opposition to positions I've just explained, which I myself detest (I've also had them scream at me about positions I like). If a teacher won't summon the imagination to place himself in the mindset of an uncongenial position he is, to that degree, behaving unethically. I know that by saying this I don't make myself popular. It runs against human impulse. But a demand of ethical behavior is, at times, to resist impulse and to act in accordance with thought-out principles.

A significant portion of professors are blatantly ideological and will advertise themselves to students as "_____ist" teachers of some sort or other.

This is oxymoronic, but it's probably less harmful than covert biases that are to a certain extent unconscious and operate not only in advocacy studies but throughout the curriculum.

Years ago I attended a class on George Eliot's novel *Middlemarch*. The teacher, a young woman recently out of graduate school, spent a good portion of her disquisition on what Dorothea Brooke, the novel's heroine, must have thought and done "as a Victorian woman." The subtext was that the Victorian woman was oppressed, whatever that might mean (I'll get to the horrors of abstraction next time), and therefore that most of Dorothea's actions had to have been colored by that oppression.

After class, while chatting with the instructor, I mentioned that we don't need to speculate about what Dorothea would have done as a Victorian woman. We know, in fact, every single thing she did, and thought, because she exists completely in the pages of the novel. If we want to talk about her responses, we need to relate them to the events she actually experienced. And we know about these events in the same way we know about her thoughts and feelings—by careful attention to the text.

These remarks appeared to startle my young colleague. She admitted, hesitantly, that she was more interested in Dorothea as a social type than as a literary character. I reminded her that if her interest lay in Victorian women there is much evidence available about women who actually lived and died during the nineteenth century. But, like all historical testimony, it points to complexity and diversity that doesn't usually fit well with any single interpretation. She said she knew, that she didn't want to be a historian, she wanted to be a literary scholar.

The truth was that she wanted to be neither historian nor literary scholar. Rather she wanted to make a point about a social role she chose to call oppression. This she had every right to do, but she should have done it straightforwardly. She could have used examples from history and literature to illustrate her argument and stayed well within the borders of ethical behavior. But, when one pretends to be helping students read a book for their own benefit— for what they can get out of it— she has no right to twist the book to fit her own political predilections. Such manipulation doesn't help students read well. In fact, it tends to make them into bad readers, and there's nothing ethical about that. It's true that this particular teacher didn't know any better. The people who had exercised academic authority over her had taught her to do as she did. Her blame personally for doing it was low, but, nonetheless, the effect was harmful.

There's a latitudinarian notion afloat in the academy that because we believe in freedom of thought and expression we are obliged to tolerate error. But just because we are required by academic decency to give all theories a forum does not mean that we have to tolerate every one of them. What, after all, does tolerate mean? My dictionary gives as its first definition "to allow without prohibiting or opposing." To say that we should not oppose error is to turn the university into a gaggle of quacking ducks whose cacophony is of no consequence. I'm afraid that's how it's seen already by a goodly portion of the public.

Ideological teaching is destructive not only because it tends to be rife with error but because it deprives students of more rewarding lessons they might gain from the materials they examine. In the example I've given here my associate was trying to carry George Eliot in her pocket to be brought out at opportune times during political campaigns. There's nothing wrong with that so long as one is open about being a campaigner, but it becomes terribly wrong when students are led to believe that George Eliot has been defined by that use. She was a fine writer and a great soul whom we, as teachers and learners, ought to approach in a spirit of respect. The first element of respect is paying attention to what she had to say. Though it's true that each reader necessarily gets a distinctive message from an encounter with a writer (depending on what he or she brings to the text), it's also true that a richer, finer reading will occur when the text is met respectfully and with a determination not to violate the boundaries of meaning it has set for itself.

It's fine, rich, reading that ideological approaches emasculate. There's little adventure in reading done for the purpose of pushing a cause. In that case the essentials needed to be known are known already. Nothing cripples learning more thoroughly than a belief that the fundamental questions have been answered. People who know everything have no need of education.

In a letter of October 28, 1865, to her friend Sarah Hennell, George Eliot remarked, "But it seems to me much better to read a man's own writings than to read what others say about him. Especially when the man is first-rate and the 'others' are third-rate." She was referring to a just-published book by David Masson on recent British philosophy and was taking exception to one of his interpretations which she said might as well have been conveyed by "a dozen lines of jargon." Add an ideological coloration to a reading and then we're unlikely to get anything even as good as a third-rate interpretation. Ethical teaching does not involve setting screens between students and materials worthy of their attention, however admirable the intent behind the screens may be.

I'll wind up today by noting that I've purposefully chosen a mild example to make my point here. I could have instanced the class that began with the statement, "Research has shown conclusively that all men are potential rapists." There have been more courses of that stripe offered in American universities over the past quarter-century than the public generally recognizes. But though they can be irritating and may confuse a few students, they overreach themselves in ways that fairly quickly strip away their credibility. They aren't as dangerous as the less aggressive, shallowly reasonable efforts that seek to make students think something rather than encouraging them to think for themselves. It's the latter that are pervasive in colleges nowadays, many of them taught by persons who have never stopped to think that it may not be entirely right to take a student's money in return for trying to shove his mind into a mold.

Next time, I'll go on to an ethical violation that will tax my powers of explanation even more than ideology has. Until then.

The sins of abstraction are doubtless the distinctive vice of our time, and nowhere are they practiced with more oily unction than in the seats of higher learning.

WILLIAM TORREY HARRIS, who was the U. S. Commissioner of Education from 1889 to 1906, regularly argued for "self-alienation" as an important element of an educational program. People needed, he said, to be taken out of their familiar habits and ways of doing things in order to return to them with a fresh eye and an enhanced comprehension of what really happens in everyday life. Harris was mainly addressing the requirement to learn about distant times and places, but I think his advice should be applied more broadly than, perhaps, he envisioned. It would help us all, now and again, to step back from ordinary modes of speech to see if we can discover how they might be viewed by someone who didn't take them for granted. In our age of wheedling verbal behavior, the need for verbal perspective is so intense that ignoring it violates ethics we should expect from any teacher.

The scandal of discipline-driven practice in the modern university is that many professors not only fail to help students step back, they work like demons to grab them by the scruffs of their necks and stick them so far into specialized verbal environments they can never get out. And they're successful too, particularly if they can hold on to a student all the way through graduate training. The speech of professors, as professors, is degraded by so many unexamined abstractions it's hard to know what they're talking about. The rationale for this kind of language is that it's addressed to an in-group and promotes professional discourse. But though it is addressed to an in-group, discourse is rarely the result. If you ask a professor what's actually meant by a colleague's abstruse comment, he usually doesn't know any better than anyone else. I know, because I've gotten into trouble by asking such questions hundreds of times. I haven't received many clear answers.

Here, for example, is a passage from a book on Shakespeare by Linda Charnes, a professor of English at Indiana University, who is regarded as a star of the literary theory movement:

> Mass culture is being increasingly "quilted," to use Lacan's term, by the *points de capiton* of what I would call the "apparitional historical." It is therefore no accident that *Hamlet* is the play to which contemporary culture most frequently returns. Hamlet the prince has come to stand for the dilemma of historicity itself.

You may not have known that Hamlet now stands for the dilemma of historicity, and if not, pooh on you. But even in your (and my) simple-minded state you can find some interesting features in this passage. We have a series of abstractions which are, in themselves, hard to pin down. They may mean one thing, they may mean another, and, at times, the ignoble suspicion creeps in that they may mean nothing at all. But the fuzziness of each one separately seems as nothing compared to the fuzziness which emerges as we try to put them into relationship with one another. Think of it: because mass culture is being quilted by quilting stitches (that's what *points de capiton* are) which really ought to be called the apparitional historical, *Hamlet* is popular, and that, in turn is true because the character Hamlet stands for the dilemma of historicity. Even if we limit ourselves to the most commonplace definitions of the words used here, we're still going to be in trouble. "Historicity" means accuracy about the past, and evidently there is a dilemma about this accuracy, a dilemma which Hamlet now represents. Does this mean simply that there are events in the past we can't know the full truth about because we have conflicting evidence? And is the play *Hamlet* really popular because all of a sudden we've realized that we can't know the full truth of the past, and that bothers us? I don't know. I could go on for a long time wondering about all this, but the question that comes to me is why should I have to? I'm tempted to recommend Ms. Charnes to Andrew Marvell and the opening lines of his most famous poem:

> Had we but world enough, and time,
> This coyness, lady, were no crime.

The truth, I'm afraid, is that Ms. Charnes is not as interested in saying something as she is in spreading an aura over her words. It's the aura that speaks more than the words, and what does the aura say? "Look at me. I'm a deep-thinker who is fully conversant with the diction of my profession. I richly deserve professional standing." Maybe she does, but where is poor Shakespeare in all this? I'm led to quote again, this time William Hazlitt, from his essay titled, "On the Ignorance of the Learned":

> If we wish to know the force of human genius we should read Shakespear. If we wish to see the insignificance of human learning we may study his commentators.

Hazlitt offers us an explanation for why unnecessary abstraction is so common: "There is a certain kind and degree of intellect in which words take root, but into which things have not power to penetrate." I'm pretty sure he was referring to abstract words and to the habit of resting content with them alone rather than burrowing behind to find the things for which they stand. Pursue this habit long enough and you'll forget that there is anything behind. The abstractions become not referents but the truth itself, or at least as much of the truth as one wishes to know.

As far as I can tell there are two prime motives for this rush to abstraction. The first is simple ease. It's much less difficult to take a general swipe at meaning than actually to hit it. I'm reminded of a current television commercial which depicts a climatic moment in a golf tournament. The golfer is lining up to make a crucial putt. He tests the wind. He studies the lay of the green. Finally, he taps the ball towards the hole; it rolls about half-way there and dies. Immediately the crowd erupts in cheering and the TV announcer booms triumphantly, "Close enough!" Fortunately, that's not true of the rules of golf, but it is increasingly true of the rules of common talk.

Years ago I was in a bookstore scanning the sales table. A lady across from me looked up and said pleasantly, "I just love to read, don't you?"

"Read what?" I asked.
"Oh, you know. Books, and like that."

Her take on reading was pretty much the same as the policy of the program in which I used to teach. There, the reading of a certain number of books is specified in order for a student to receive credit. Students have repeatedly asked what the program means by a "book." But they get no official answer. Technically, *Jonathan Livingston Seagull* counts the same as the *Critique of Pure Reason*. Occasionally, some faculty members will acknowledge the problems created by such vagueness and suggest that the reading requirement be spelled out more specifically—by numbers of words, or pages, or even levels of complexity. But, it's just too hard, so nobody does anything about it.

This, by the way, is of benefit to the degree salesmen in their guise as admissions officers. When talking to prospective students they can try to close the sale by conveying—guardedly, of course, but also truthfully—that students are not required to take up materials that might tax their minds.

Laziness is reprehensible and can lead to ethical transgressions, but it's not as bad as the second main motive behind excessive abstraction: the desire to control people by deception. There's a vast literature on the topic. Though there have been many good recent treatments (I'm fond, for example, of Ian Hacking's *The Social Construction of What?*, which gets at the topic in an interesting way), the champion in the field is probably still George Orwell's essay, "Politics and the English Language."

Orwell laid out the nature of deceptive language graphically. His description came directly from what he read in his daily newspapers, but accurate as his observations were then they're even more accurate now. Language, especially the language of the schools, has continued to decay since he wrote fifty-four years ago. Here's a key passage that shows his prescience:

> In our age there is no such thing as "keeping out of politics." All issues are political issues, and politics itself is a mass of lies, evasions, folly, hatred and schizophrenia. When the general atmosphere is bad, language must suffer.

When we talk and write as politicians, or, as Orwell would put it, as publicists trying to dupe people, we use words not to tell the truth or to make our meaning clear, but to deceive and mislead. We want to make people do what we want them to without their recognizing what's happening. Unaware victims are always more pliant.

I recall years ago reading an essay by—I think—the British critic Clive James in which he said that if you describe things as being better than they are, you'll be called an optimist, and if you describe things as worse than they are, you'll be called a pessimist, but if you describe things exactly as they are, you'll be called insane. I've tested the proposition since then and generally found it to be true. The one thing the control mongers of the world cannot abide is to hear things spoken of as they are. That's because there's no profit in it for them. They have to paint the things that enhance their power as wonderful and the things that threaten it as horrendous. Otherwise, they couldn't keep the rest of us jumping through their hoops.

The world is awash in deceitful language, and much of it takes the form of noble-sounding abstractions which cover despicable behavior. Just think of them: a phalanx composed merely of "business ethics," "customer service," "debt consolidation," "drug education," "recovered memory," "terrorist," "think tank," and "development" is itself enough to keep a good portion of the world in thralldom. I, myself, have heard the latter deployed in so many noxious ways I almost feel I should pitch a fit whenever it comes out of anyone's mouth. What I really should do is begin a campaign to have it listed in dictionaries with a proper modern definition, something like:

> a word, along with its derivatives, which infects its users with sleazy behavior, whether it's applied to throwing up unsightly and unneeded office complexes, screwing money out of donors for already engorged universities, professionalizing oneself by discovering the astounding fact that big kids can do things little kids can't do, or helping psychologists induce people to give up their ideals.

C. S. Lewis, in his interesting little book *The Abolition of Man,* has this to say about the ethical responsibilities of a good teacher:

> For every one pupil who needs to be guarded from a weak excess of sensibility there are three who need to be awakened from the slumber of cold vulgarity. The task of the modern educator is not to cut down jungles but to irrigate deserts.

"Cold vulgarity" is a good term for designating the false, dried-up abstractions which abound throughout the academy today. It doesn't matter whether they come from the philistine precincts of "management studies" or the pretensions of literary theory. Their effect is to cut students off from direct encounter with words and events that can stir their souls and turn their minds towards the specific interactions that give life its fascination. It's the duty of teachers to help students fight their way through the thickets of institutionalized obfuscation. When they don't do it, when they give their first loyalty to institutional structures of reward rather than to the education of their students, they are failing ethically.

Next time I'll take up a third moral duty teachers ought to be more aware of than they are now.

My third ethic addresses the teacher's duty to confront the simplicities of popular culture, particularly where, as in America now, the popular culture is obsessed with winning and losing, success and failure, right and wrong.

MY THIRD ETHIC for educators takes up a problem that may be harder for Americans to comprehend than it is for other people. In this country we are addicted to victory, to being, as we say, number one. As a consequence, we have a hard time imagining that any significant activity should not be subservient to victory or that any feature of a losing side might have something to be said for it. This can be an energizing stance and it has its uses, particularly if we conceive of life as a game or a contest. But it's not a mindset that supports education because the purpose of education is not winning but learning.

I'm grateful that the House Committee on Un-American Activities has passed beyond its tenure. Otherwise I might be hauled before it for saying such a thing. Still, it's true. In education we don't confront challenges in order to vanquish them or to win out over our opponents. We face up to them in order to learn from them.

Over the past decade, as I've listened to students express their ambitions, few of them have spoken of a desire to deepen their essential understanding. It's as though people have lost the ability to imagine learning anything new of fundamental value. They seem to believe their current grasp of the human situation is not only adequate but unquestionable, so that for them schooling becomes a matter of picking up a few techniques that might afford a competitive edge.

This is the most anti-educational attitude one can have. It's the duty of educators to find ways to modify it, to help students think about what they don't understand rather than what they do. In no duty does the current set of professors fail more miserably. Instead of challenging students to step outside their present assumptions and to view life from broader perspectives, the majority of teachers I've observed either encourage students to indulge themselves in their narrowness or seek to replace one set of narrow beliefs with another just as straitened. It's not education to persuade an absolutist to adopt a different absolutism. Nothing is gained by shifting from one cock-sure stupidity to another. The difference between Brand A of ideology and Brand B is like the difference between a louse and a flea.

I may seem to be repeating what I said in my first ethic, but I think there's a distinction between the argument of the sixteenth letter and this one. There I was countering the presumption of imposing one's own beliefs on students. Here, I want to refute the idea that a person's intellectual options are limited to publicly proclaimed postures or to conventionally right solutions. Some of us have got it in our heads that since politics invades all corners of institutional life we have to surrender our own minds to political puritanism.

During the campus unrest of the 1970s, I recall a Yale professor saying with respect to one set of student radicals that there's nothing sadder than a group of people who believe their own bullshit. Just think how horrible it would be if either of the two current political parties actually believes all the stuff it spouts on the campaign trail. Every now and then I have a waking nightmare that both do, and then I despair for my country. You know how people are always saying they want politicians to keep their promises? What can they be thinking of? I'd ten times rather have a politician with the education to think through a situation than one who rigidly sacrificed the public good to honor foolish campaign pledges or to do in the opposing party. It may be, though, that education has become politicized to the extent that many (with politicians among the leaders) have lost the discernment to see it as an activity with its own demands and morality. They are so obsessed with pushing a position they forget that education declines to push anything—except maybe itself—in order to be free to examine everything.

I occasionally recall the Clarence Thomas-Anita Hill frenzy of 1991 as an example of how astute speculation has been driven from public discourse. A decade ago in that case everyone seemed forced to take a side. One of the two principals had to be telling the truth and the other had to be lying. One was pure and the other was disgusting. This was the political conclusion. But from an educated perspective there were other possibilities as likely as the two that were foisted on us everyday by the combatants.

When two people disagree over something that occurred between them, we ought to reflect that each may be exaggerating. Each may be telling some portion of the truth, and each may be shading the truth to advance his or her own contention. Furthermore, each may be doing it sincerely, believing his or her own story, and certainly believing in his or her own rectitude. Politics insists on everything being simple. It wants heroes and villains. Education, by contrast, knows that almost nothing is as simple as it seems.

I wish I knew more about the source of this Manichaeism, this dualism, this two-sidedness in public thought. Perhaps its arises from intellectual laziness. It's easier to think the truth lies all here, or all there, than to dig it out from the fissures where it habitually secretes itself. But to assign the dichotomized mind to laziness alone would be to commit the sin I'm trying to refute. It probably oozes out of more places than anybody could ever list.

One support, clearly, is the American judicial system, with its concept that two adversaries, each presenting only the portion of the truth that's favorable to its cause, offers the best avenue to right action. It strikes me as a dubious proposition. Yet my poor brain is taxed sufficiently by trying to define education that I can't be straying off into other areas. It might take another lifetime to delve into criminal justice. I'll say only that its effect on educational thinking has been less than helpful.

Another source has been a melodramatic popular culture with its pantheon of heroes and villains. When James Bond goes up against Goldfinger, there's little call for an educated mind to sort out the rights and wrongs of the situation. I will say, though, that some elements of popular culture are coming round to more nuanced understandings of motivation and circumstance than you'll see laid out on the Dan Rather Show. The legal drama *Law and Order*, for example, has a set of principal characters who are often as villainous as they are admirable. A fascinating question concerning the series is what portion of the audience grasps the subtleties it is being offered and what percentage is as blind as the protagonists are. In any case, the show gives us conflicts that require some thought, and that can only be good for education.

The geo-political situation that prevailed over most of our adult lives had a dampening effect on careful thought. The notion of a "Cold War" in which the "Free World" opposed an "Evil Empire" did more harm than historians will be able to tally over the next century. Even with the demise of the Soviet Union its effects linger. Scarcely a week passes without a letter to my local paper denouncing something or other as communistic. The writer generally has no idea what the word means and employs it simply to denounce without taking on the bother of thinking why his target deserves denunciation. We can say that blather of that kind is merely evidence of stupidity. And we would be right. Still, stupidity takes different forms at different times. We have the responsibility to ask why in America nowadays it mostly shows itself as over-simplified, black-white thinking.

As I said, it would be impossible to run through all the causes, but the one I'm going to end with today deserves special attention both because it has been largely ignored by the public and because it involves, probably, the deepest irony of our recent history.

I have in mind the consequences of "the great school wars," that is, the debate about the proper function of public schooling among the professionals who claim to have dedicated themselves to education. I've just finished reading Diane Ravitch's *Left Back: A Century of Failed School Reforms.*

In it she chronicles the arguments that have taken place among university theorists during the 20th century over what the schools should be doing. It is a gripping and a dismal story.

Before I move on to some of Ms. Ravitch's findings I need to inject a digression on the hijacking of a word. Throughout the nation, the academic units that attempt to instruct aspiring teachers on how to teach are called departments of education. I can think of no greater verbal transgression. Even if these departments were behaving sensibly they wouldn't deserve the title. Education is the function of the entire university, not just of a single department. These units should be called departments of pedagogy because that's what they are.

The irony arises from the truth that a goodly percentage of the inhabitants of these departments are refugees from education. They entered college and discovered they didn't have the curiosity or vigor of mind to pursue literature, history, physical science, or mathematics, and so they fled into "education." They became educationists because they disliked education and wanted to turn it into something else.

I realize there are numerous exceptions to what I've just said, many people who pursued degrees from departments of education because they genuinely cared about strengthening teaching and learning in the schools. They deserve our respect. Yet, it seems fairly clear that in their own bailiwicks they have been in the minority. If we go out amongst the "interlocking directorate," identified by historian Arthur Bestor, Jr. in the 1950s, made up of professors of education, school administrators, and bureaucrats in state and federal education agencies, we find few people who love knowledge or who put their faith in processes of careful thought. If one needs evidence about their intellectual character he can turn to the literature they produce. It is dreadfully cloudy, clotted and abstract, showing no respect for the beauty of words. Virtually all of it deserves the judgment rendered by Dick Feagler, a columnist for the Cleveland *Plain Dealer*, speaking of a report by an educational reform group: "English is a second language for the members of the National Council of Teachers of English. Their primary language is gobbledygook."

Diane Ravitch's central thesis is that theorists who were hostile to academic pursuits dominated the national debate over the schools from the 1920s until recently. Reacting against what they saw as rigid, unimaginative, and stultifying teaching they decided that everything the schools had stood for up till their time was bad and had to be discarded. Though they introduced a number of healthy pedagogical reforms, they also turned against the traditional curricula of literature, history, science and mathematics, and through a dizzying sequence of movements attempted to replace them with various economic and psychological training programs. There was the vocational education movement, the social efficiency movement, the mental measurement movement, the child-centered movement, the activity movement, the curriculum revision movement, the mental hygiene movement, the social reconstruction movement. Though all these programs deemed themselves "progressive," the only thing they had in common was hostility towards liberal learning. They did not believe that all children need to be taught to read, calculate, and think at levels beyond the elementary, and they certainly did not believe that all children are capable of understanding the human cultural heritage and making intelligent choices about how to integrate it into their personal lives. Diane Ravitch believes passionately that every student does deserve these things and that any decent democracy will attempt to provide them through a common curriculum that doesn't discriminate against any child based on somebody's test or somebody's theory about what he or she is capable of doing in later life.

I agree with her heartily, but my point in citing her here is not agreement as much as an attempt to show how a "movement" mentality has afflicted higher education. People who believe in movements tend to hold that old things, whatever they are, need to be got rid of completely. The old thing is bad. The new thing is good. This is Manichaeism with a vengeance, and it is always hostile to educated thinking which deals in shades, nuances, and incremental differences. Students deserve to be taught how to make ever finer discriminations. When their teachers fail to make that effort, they are also failing in their ethical duty.

These last three letters have been such a scanty treatment of a vast subject I'm embarrassed by them. But I can excuse myself somewhat when I recall that I didn't set out to "cover" educational ethics. I wanted merely to point out that they exist independently of other ethics and have their being and identity in the activity they are designed to serve. Next time, on to another topic.

This is the fuzziest letter of the set. The thing I'm searching for is subtle; it doesn't bang itself into your head instantaneously. And I think you have to understand something of its nature before you can give it the value it deserves.

AFTER TAKING A brief furlough from these letters to do a couple other things, I'm ready to start back and begin the second half of the series. It's a good point for self-reflection: to ask myself what my purposes are and to inquire about the nature of the definition I'm chasing.

"Why didn't you do that at the start?" a critic might complain. My answer would be that it wasn't possible. Education is one of those curious qualities that can't be described until you've worked your way into its vicinity. If you try to define it from long distance, you're reduced to the platitudes that appear in the introductions to college catalogues and are so vacuous no one pays them any mind. They may be true, but their truth has no bite.

The first eighteen letters can be seen as an effort to get in the neighborhood of education so that in the second eighteen we can track it to its lair.

I'm not interested merely in adding yet one more critique of colleges and universities. Their corruption by the forces of mammon is so widely understood you can scarcely get an argument about it anymore, except from the degree salesmen, who testify as any other set of hucksters would. Giving them credence would be like believing a car salesman who told you his product was going to transform your self-image and take care of your blood pressure besides. The flood of books detailing the university's corruption— I got two in my mailbox just last week: Bill Reading's *The University in Ruins* and Christopher Lucas's *Crisis in the Academy* —shows us that bringing the rottenness to light doesn't by itself lead to improvement. Knowing you're on the wrong path is something, but it doesn't automatically tell you where the right path is.

I have said the right path involves putting education at the center of the university's concerns. Yet, saying so doesn't help much unless one can define education clearly enough for people to be able to take hold of it. Although I've made a beginning, I need now to say more about the character of the definition I'm seeking so that I don't mislead you or anybody else.

"Education" is a word with several legitimate definitions—legitimate at least when we're talking loosely. In addition to its definitions it's also encrusted with a host of associated qualities which are thought to be so tightly bonded with it that it never appears independently of them. With all these secondary definitions and associations it's hard to get a clear view of the thing itself. Yet, it is the thing itself that I want to concentrate on and that I would like to see at the core of the university's self-image. The associated things can be all right. Some of them are admirable. Focusing on them, however, causes us to lose sight of the ideal the university cannot neglect if it is to be worthy of its name.

I realize I'm getting into deep philosophical thickets, and that I may not be philosopher enough to clear them all away. The thing itself? What am I talking about? Is there any such thing? What is this education in itself I'm trying to define and serve?

I'm running against intellectual fashion in trying to answer. Post-modern voices tell us there is no thing in itself behind words, that language is a vast interaction among words which refers to nothing but itself. But this is just ingenuity playing games with reality. One finally has to live by what he has seen. I've actually seen education happen to people. I like the results, and I want to live in a world where it happens more often than it does now. My doubts don't relate to education's existence but to my puny powers of explanation. But just because you're unsure of your power to do your duty doesn't mean it's gone away.

There are physical objects, and physical actions, and concepts, and ideas, and fancies, and dreams, and hopes, and hypotheses, and notions. The trouble with education is it's not any one of these. That's what makes it so damned hard to talk about. I'm not sure what we can say education is in the abstract. The closest I can come is to call it an experience of a certain sort which produces pleasure of a certain sort, but a pleasure accompanied by pangs. The qualifier "of a certain sort" sets me my task in the remainder of these letters. What sort of experience is education? What sort of pleasure does it produce? And what are the pangs that necessarily go along with it?

As you know, I've been fond of quoting R. G. Collingwood's warning that people who use words to mean what they don't really mean are poisoning the well of civilization. I have no wish to be a poisoner. I don't want to give education a definition out of line with the definitions in dictionaries. But I do want to extract from those definitions their core meaning, and then develop it so we can see how the university might serve it more honorably than it has up till now.

Remember I mentioned Tennyson's remark about life's encounters?

> All experience is an arch wherethro'
> Gleams that untravell'd world whose margin fades
> For ever and for ever when I move.

If all experience is that way we shouldn't expect education to be different, and, in fact, it's not. It's a gleaming, moving thing. We get whiffs and touches of it, but we don't ever seal it up in a box. I said this earlier but I see no harm in saying it again. When we get down to the actions we can take, what we're looking for are the things we can do that are most likely to offer us the whiffs.

The best known adage about higher education in America used to be expressed by the image of Mark Hopkins on one end of a log and a student on the other. I don't know much about Mark Hopkins except that for a long time he was a professor of moral philosophy and rhetoric at Williams College. But even that bit hints at the definition I'm pursuing. Moral philosophy and rhetoric are good topics for anyone who wants to be serious about education. Along with physical science and mathematics they come close to covering all an undergraduate needs. That they have been replaced by the smorgasbord of subjects that now make up the college curriculum emphasizes the problem we're facing. The cancerous explosion of departments and majors that has come about since Hopkins was at Williams shows how colleges have metastasized from institutions that at least made a bow to education to things that are impossible to understand until we recall that they reek throughout of lucre. I was reminded of the current situation a few nights ago watching *Ally McBeal*. One of the characters, Lin, was explaining how she keeps men interested. During the day at work she tapes hundred dollar bills to the intimate parts of her body. Then at night, when her boyfriend seeks her out in bed, she smells of money. "Hell," I thought to myself, "she would make a great candidate for the next president of any of the colleges I've worked for."

What Hopkins and the student talked about on the log, though, is less important than the log itself: a place where people come together to engage in back and forth with a desire to learn from one another. This is the key ingredient of education, the *sine qua non*, so much so we can say that where it's taking place, there education is, and where it is not, education has fled. I don't think most people grasp how little discourse goes on within the halls of universities. There's incessant talk, of course: gossip without limitation— who's in and who's out, who got what grant, what book contract. There's endless proselytism, preaching on topics more bizarre than most people have heard of. There's an obsession with money that's heart-deadening. But let a real discourse develop, where the participants are forced to deal honestly with one another's perceptions, and most university folk will discover urgent business calling them elsewhere. If I had a dollar for all the professors I've seen run away from conversations that pushed too close to their pet hypotheses, I could be sending you these letters on gold foil—though, come to think of it, that probably wouldn't make them any better.

From the point of view of the degree salesmen, the only thing to be said about discourse is that it's expensive. What they want are systems—schemes that can be wrapped in fancy packages and sold for five, ten, fifteen times the cost of producing them. This is the reason for the rush to so-called distance learning. It lends itself to schematics and avoids the cost of putting bodies in rooms face to face.

We should be skeptical of reducing education to systems not only because they're insipid but because observation teaches us that when they're tried the results are puny. I realize I'm standing up here for something that can be abused. But just because the truth can be twisted doesn't mean we should abandon it. I know there are people who have taken education's non-systematic nature and used it as an excuse to be self-indulgent and sloppy. The entire history of a college I used to be part of was shaped by that practice. When I was there and saw it in action I got just as angry as the most hard-headed positivist. Even so, the truth of the arts of learning remains that they have to be spontaneous and open to interpretation based on individual experience. Remove the elements of personal freedom from the liberal arts and they become either fatuous or tools of propaganda. This means, in practice, that education has to be pursued through give and take, and that no prediction can be made in advance about where educational discourse will lead.

Every now and then on a board of trustees a fathead will arise and announce that the university is a business and must be run in accordance with business principles. This is the reason why some form of intellectual independence for faculty members is essential. Otherwise inquiry would be throttled by officials who have never glimpsed education and wouldn't know it if it were stuck in front of them.

The university is not only not a business. It is in many respects the opposite of a business. A good businessman knows exactly where he's going. The teacher who knows exactly where he's going with his students has committed heresy. He has turned his students into the ingredients of a system and has deserted them as moral and intellectual agents in themselves. Mr. Lincoln warned us that a house divided against itself cannot stand, and that's precisely the situation of a university that seeks to become a business. It may be successful in its own terms, but in the process it will have got out of the business (to use an oxymoron) of education.

I'm now brought to the feature of my definition I'm most hesitant to introduce. My hesitancy has nothing to do with doubts about what I must say. It comes from knowing I'll be opening myself to charges of sentimentality and ridiculousness, especially from the degree salesmen. But since I haven't been very skilled up till now in avoiding their ridicule, I don't guess there's sense in trying to start at this late date. So, I'll be blatant and say that unless an activity is charged with faith, it is not education.

In Tolstoy's novel *Anna Karenina* there's a minor character named Mikhaylov, a painter who has migrated from Russia to Italy, who's presented as being a freethinker, but not in the old style of someone who has digested the authorities and decided to take a stance independent of them. No, this Mikhaylov is unaware that there ever were laws of religion and morality, however flawed. He is, in the words of one of my translations, "a heathen" and in another, "an utter savage." He has never imagined, as Thomas Carlyle put it, that in the dead husks of the creeds there might be something that can legitimately called faith.

Mikhaylov reminds me of many of the persons currently in charge of universities. They have no knowledge of the struggles of the past and, therefore, no faith in the sacredness of education's essence. They have not imagined that it exists. They use the word "education," of course. They use it repeatedly. But they don't apply it to that glimmering goal of intelligent discourse and imaginative perception that gives the world its legitimacy. Instead, they apply it to things that are not education. Because they do it repeatedly, and because they are decked with the robes of authority, which they don't hesitate to exploit, they drive the genuine thing-in-itself out of the university. They don't do it because they dislike education. They do it because they don't know it exists and they can't imagine a reason to find out what it is.

If this sounds radically Platonic, so be it. It would be a comfort not to have to say these things. But I've watched education being mis-served for so long I can't pretend its treatment in the universities is the result of ordinary human imperfection—not when I know it comes from extraordinary intellectual callowness.

I haven't yet explained the thing-in-itself I set out to define. That's why I have more letters to write. I hope this one hasn't repeated unnecessarily things I said before. I had to re-emphasize features of earlier letters to make the point that education is an experience in itself, and that though we may not be able to define it with perfect precision we can know it with sufficient assurance to keep on its trail. That's the main thing I wanted to say this time. Now I can go on to a series of comparisons that will sketch it more clearly than I have till now.

Chief among the things education is not is the pursuit of money. Here I try to explain that though quests for money and education can sometimes support one another, the two motivations are, in their essence, near opposites.

*I*N THIS LETTER, along with the next two, I want to point out how education is different from activities that are generally confused with it. When I first considered this section, I thought I would need a lengthy series of comparisons to clarify the mixed up nature of public discourse on this topic. But, on reflection, I've decided that three will be enough to suggest how others might be made.

I'll begin with one that would occur to anybody who has thought much about education. It's the one a fair number of college professors recognize and deplore. It's the one politicians most often pontificate about. I'm referring to the habit of seeing education as a preparation for making money.

I may be giving some readers the feeling that I'm down on money. But, I'm not. I like it as much as I do most things, and I certainly wish I had more of it than I do. I differ from some of my fellow citizens, and the degree salesmen, in that I don't like it more than anything, nor do I believe it's a proper object of worship.

Education is one of the things I set above money because it brings greater pleasure and because it's possessed of greater potential than money is. If everybody in the world were suddenly to become rich (a logical impossibility, I know) our affairs would be different, but they wouldn't be morally transformed. The totality of nastiness might change its form but probably not its volume. On the other hand, if everyone should start pursuing education, we would gain a brighter world overnight.

As soon as you face the truth that the effects of two things are different you can no longer believe that the things themselves are the same, nor can you believe that getting one translates perfectly into getting the other. Given the astoundingly disparate consequences of money and education, it makes no sense to think that you get the one in order to get the other. Neither does it make sense to say that preparation to get one *is* the other. Yet, that's exactly what many of our social and political leaders come on the television everyday and tell us. They are, as Collingwood warned, poisoning the well of civilization.

Confusion about the difference between things comes about because people don't stop to think what each is. Money, after all, is a fairly simple thing. It's the power to cause other people to behave as you want them to. You can get bodies with money, and you can get them to do just about anything you can imagine (as long as it falls within the realm of possibility). In as far as money is concerned, your relationship with all other people is as a self to mechanisms—rather ingenious mechanisms to be sure, but mechanisms all the same.

In 1973, a movie came out that was to become fairly famous, written and directed by Michael Crichton, called *Westworld*. It told the story of a batch of entrepreneurs who had created extremely lifelike robots, machines that looked like people, talked like people, and—what was perhaps most important—felt like people. These robots had been set up in fantasy worlds that mimicked historical settings. You could—for a hefty fee—go to wild west world, or Roman world, or medieval world, and hang out there as long as you liked. One of the compelling sales features of these worlds was that the female robots were amazingly compliant. You could go to medieval world, for example, and say, "Come here wench," and she would come and do anything you wanted her to.

I've talked to guys who thought that would be endlessly delightful. But, truth is, the pleasure it offered would have about the same staying power as the new academic programs being gussied up by the degree salesmen for delivery over the internet. The reason is the same in both cases: reality offers stronger rewards than illusion. Try as you will to convince yourself that a machine woman is, for all practical purposes, the same as a real woman, it's not true. There's something in us that demands shared experiences with persons like ourselves. Relationships engineered by money, even if they're with real people, are in the direction of the relationship you would have with one of the robot women of medieval world. There can be no living communion involved because money will strangle it. Obviously, interactions initiated by money can turn into something else. We've all learned that from watching *Pretty Woman*. But they have to change, they have to shed the cash nexus before they can become humanly real.

Education is a process whereby minds encounter other minds. It's different from the money process where minds use bodies (or their products). I'll admit that the two sometimes get mixed up. How could it be otherwise in a money-crazed society like ours? Even so, it's not difficult to see which part of a relationship is which, or to understand that what happens in a true meeting of minds cannot be reduced to an exchange of money. This being the case, how can anyone define education as preparation to make money? Money itself tends to operate as a barrier to mental exchange. And surely, no one would consciously argue that education can take place without an interaction between minds?

I say so, but, of course, that's exactly what the degree salesmen do argue, if not consciously, at least by implication. Most of their money-making schemes involve reducing the mind-to-mind interactions in college work and replacing them with mechanical (and now, electronic) injections of one sort or another. How they can believe in this is difficult to understand. I don't have much of an explanation myself, because try as I will to have exchanges with the degree salesmen (or at least their local representatives) I haven't found a way. They don't converse; they don't write; they don't offer considered theories of education. They're too busy making money which is, after all, the gravamen of all their arguments, the "bottom line."

When I was a child I would often hear, as I suppose all children hear, that money is the root of all evil. This was perplexing to me because the same people who said it seemed to be chasing money like starved dogs after raw meat. My father often talked at me about money. He hurled supposedly money-wise adages at me as though I was a kewpie doll at the county fair. Yet, on those rare occasions when I would try to talk to him about what money was really worth, he would just shake his head and turn away. I think that gave me my first inkling that money had some peculiarly estranging power that held people back from sharing their thoughts with one another.

My father and I never had a real conversation. During his final days, when you would think the power of money would have relaxed its grip, he continued to harangue me about it. I recall one time, about ten days before he died, while he was in the midst of a long, seemingly crazed denunciation of me for having spent money on something he disapproved of—perhaps a book— when he paused, and an expression came on his face I had not seen before. Then he said, "Well, I suppose you've been a pretty good son." It was the only compliment I ever got from him in my life. The irony is that it came at a time when he may have been so demented it meant nothing.

All the way through my life I've watched money erect the same wall between people that it threw up between me and my father. It has persuaded people whom I generally thought well of to do amazingly mean-spirited things, even when only small amounts of it were at stake. I've seen men who wouldn't think of kicking a dog take away the ability of families to live decently, not out of genuine financial exigency, but just because money was crying out to maximize itself, to grow by fifteen percent rather than by ten.

At some point an educated person in this society has to face the truth that money has become more than an instrument. It exists as a social talisman whose powers of mystical elevation transcend anything one might buy with it.

During the final ten years of his life my father struggled with a worn out lawnmower, which became progressively less efficient and, finally, dangerous. Every time I urged him to get a new one, I got the same rejoinder: "Don't you know that lawnmowers cost money?" He was never a rich man, but during his later years he had accumulated more than enough to live comfortably if he had been willing to do so. The cost of a lawnmower would have been virtually nothing to him. Yet he couldn't stand parting with the small sum it would have taken to make life more pleasant in that respect. It's a common enough story, yet its very commonness may hide its meaning.

Money tends to become not only an end in itself, but an end that seeks to crush all other ends. This is why it persists as the root of evil. It's farcical to think of education as a preliminary, as propadeutic, to money-making, because money in its pure form, as talisman rather than instrument, can't stand the idea of education. Its primacy is threatened by education, and in its religious form its own primacy is what it seeks above all else. The first commandment of every god there ever was is to forbid setting any other god ahead of it.

It may seem exaggerated to speak of money as a religion. But, look around. What's more deserving of the title? The point I'm trying to make here, about the conflict between money and education, and the corresponding illogic of equating education with preparation for making it, is addressed to money in its spiritual guise. Seen as an instrument, money is simply another tool for easing physical burdens. We spread it over life as we spread butter on toast. It's when it's hoarded for its own sake that it takes on the features of a monstrous deity, a Belial demanding human sacrifice that would nauseate for any other reason.

What else other than education can keep money from overstepping its bounds? How often do we have to watch it run amok before stopping to ask, "Wait a minute; what is this stuff anyway?" Money and its servants don't want that question asked. Their natural mode is secrecy. That's why you can't draw them into conversation. That's why they always run away to attend to their busy-ness. That's why you can't get the degree salesmen to read a book or write a letter.

The irony here is that education does assist in making money in reasonable ways and amounts. It promotes clarity, efficiency, realistic assessment—all necessary qualities for producing the goods and services of economic life. These are the by-products of education. It's when the by-products become the goal that we get into trouble.

I used to think that the primary thrust of the degree salesmen was to turn the university into a training institute for money-making organizations. Now I see I was mistaken. Though that may be their conscious purpose, little training of a useful economic sort actually occurs in universities. The corporations themselves can take care of their training needs and, in fact, now operate as extensive a network of schools as the university system itself. What they need from the university is a church. The boy who gets an undergraduate degree in management hasn't learned much to help him perform a specific job. But his belief structures have been molded. He has learned that money is the answer to all questions of why. He is spiritually prepared to dedicate his life to busy-ness. The corporation can now do with him as it will.

If you'll trace through the etymology of "education" you'll find scant warrant for defining it as a process for producing that result. Nothing that transforms a person into a servant of processes he hasn't examined can be called educative. There is no excuse for telling young people to go to college so they can get good jobs.

Next time I'll try to unravel an association that has been even more closely connected to people's notions of education than money has.

Snobbery may be one of the ineradicable sins. Certainly it's always present in scenes where prestige depends solely on being "culturally" conversant, which in current universities is valued more than education is.

MY SECOND CONTRAST between education and things that are confused with it comes from a false conception of education's motive quality. We've bought in to an educational ideal of inert reception when action is the quality we should be after. Most of those who acknowledge the value of the studies I've been discussing would call them "cultural." And in the popular mind culture is a relatively quiescent thing, a costume reserved for Sundays, holidays, and an occasional evening out. It's not a habit one employs in everyday work. It's a spice rather than a dietary substance.

In observing university communities, I've encountered lots of people who are viewed by their acquaintances as cultured or erudite. They're always up on recent books, concerts, plays, exhibitions. Not only have they heard of these things, they have a sentence or two at hand for each one of them. They're prepared to discuss anything for three minutes, but when talk runs much beyond that, their commentary begins to dry up. Beyond the judgment that the thing was stunning, or marvelous, or execrable, or derivative, or wildly provocative there seems little to be said.

Occasionally, just to be the irritant I am, I'll ask, "What did it cause you to do?" Then I get the universal expression, the amalgam of indignation and discomfiture, that tells me I've stepped over the social line. Indeed, I have. It's not a question one should ask often. There's nothing wrong with sharing bits of information about books, plays, films, or concerts. But there's nothing elevated about it either. It's no different from talking about last night's NBA game, or who got a traffic ticket, or who was seen going into a bar with whom. It's gossip, and it functions as all gossip functions, to get people out of one another's presence without the bother of having to engage in thought.

I talked once with a businessman who said he wanted his upper level managers to have studied the liberal arts so they wouldn't be embarrassed if someone mentioned Chagall or Kandinsky at a cocktail party. This is the view of culture that equates it with eye shadow, lipstick, and cuff links.

I heard a colleague last year praising the educational attainments of an academic official. He speaks more than six languages, she said. It's a pity, I replied, that he's found nothing interesting to say in any of them.

At a faculty conference several years ago somebody suggested that we all make a list of our ten favorite movies. After the first three lists had been read I realized I had not seen any of the films nor had I heard of any of them. They all seemed to have been viewed in art movie houses around Cambridge and to have been made either in Asia or Eastern Europe. There was no "The King and I," or "Red River." When conversation got underway, though, no one had much to say about the movies. The only significant thing about them appeared to be their titles, which gave people the opportunity to pronounce foreign words.

Anyone can add to my short list of culture buggery. It's endemic in certain circles. I used to think that though annoying it was harmless. But lately I've come to see it's not the benign foolishness I once thought it was. It's an evil, one that shifts rapidly back and forth between two camps. One is of a defensive character and one can be very aggressive.

When I say evil can be defensive, I'm speaking of its ability to block or screen the good, to put itself in place of genuine virtue and to convince people that it's an adequate substitute. It's then taking the form of a quackery. That's what's happening when people equate education with lazy wallowing in so-called aesthetic appreciation. Taken by itself, appreciation is a good, but not a very important one. All it offers is a pleasant way to pass time. At the risk of sounding anthropocentric I'll say that passing time is not what we are on earth to do. Certainly, if it were, we would have no need of education. If that were our purpose, education is the last thing we would want to take up.

Appreciation becomes an element of education by immersing itself in something far greater, a quality we've lost the ability to speak of in its full form because we've diluted the words that refer to it. The eighteenth century Italian philosopher Giovanni Vico argued that one of humanity's finest possessions is *fantasia,* a word that's often translated as "imagination," but which for him meant more than we generally infer from the term. For Vico, *fantasia* was the ability to enter minds different from our own and, thereby, to understand that they see what we do not see. We can do this because various as human cultures are they all fall within the boundaries of humanity; they have all been created by humans. And what one human has made, another human can understand, but usually not without hard striving. The latter is what education is, and that's why all of the astounding number of efforts to avoid it can be subsumed under the heading of intellectual laziness.

In the history of ideas, Vico is often spoken of as a precursor to the German thinker Johann Gottfried Herder, who by a curious coincidence was born in the very year (1744) that Vico died. Though Herder had not read Vico when he wrote his best known works, there must have been something in the intellectual atmosphere to suggest similar conclusions to both of them. One of Herder's central arguments was that mere contemplation yields no truth, that it is only by taking an active part in life that one can get at truth's nature. When men, as he said, "live on other men's accounts," they become superfluous cosmopolitans whose vital feelings have been drained away. It wouldn't be unreasonable to apply that description to the majority of professors in the liberal arts nowadays. Even when they recognize the corruptions being promoted by the degree salesmen, their feelings are not strong enough to raise resistance, and so they become grumbly, unwitting accomplices. If you survey the literature that modern professors put forward to justify their cushy lives, you'll see that much of it falls into a category Herder was addressing when he said, "We speak the words of strangers, and they wean us from our own thoughts." It's a judgment that has become ever more common as we have moved from Herder's time to our own, very close to what Yeats had in mind in his poem, "The Scholars":

> Bald heads, forgetful of their sins,
> Old, learned, respectable bald heads
> Edit and annotate the lines
> That young men, tossing on their beds,
> Rhymed out in love's despair
> To flatter beauty's ignorant ear.
>
> All shuffle there; all cough in ink;
> All wear the carpet with their shoes;
> All think what other people think;
> All know the man their neighbor knows.
> Lord, what would they say
> Did their Catullus walk that way?

It's a travesty of education to posit it as inert reception, as regurgitation, as appreciation, as connoisseurship. Learning which causes one to do no more than sit back and feel pleasantly superior to the hoi polloi isn't educative at all. It doesn't cause anybody to engage another mind for the sake of dialogue. In fact, it's the death of dialogue because it convinces its adherents that they know all they need to know to raise themselves above the mass. When we find people putting that sort of thing in the place of education, the results can only be bad.

That's the defensive effect of artificial cultivation, of snobbish refinement. But, I also said it had an aggressive component. To get at it we need to keep in mind that the fundamental definition of evil is the practice of viewing other people not as moral ends in themselves but as objects of one's own desire. There are people for whom cultivation serves to convince that they have earned the right to use others by reason of superior taste and refinement. This sort of thinking can operate both as personal egotism and as group privilege.

Within the vast bigotry of anti-Semitism, there has been a persistent theme portraying the Jews as inferior because of their avid pursuit of vulgar pleasures as contrasted with the pure, ethereal, cultured vision of the Aryan races. T. S. Eliot occasionally succumbed to this nonsense, as in "Gerontion," where he speaks of the Jew squatting at the window of a decaying house whose owner, an old man himself in a state of decay, has been corroded by life in the seedy capitals of Europe. There's nothing specifically anti-Semitic in Eliot's words, but the image they convey suggests a person watching for something to pounce upon, waiting to seize the smallest advantage.

In a more famous poem, "Sweeney Among the Nightingales," Eliot has "Rachel née Rabinovitch" ripping at grapes with "murderous paws." She and another woman, described only as wearing a Spanish cape, seem to be plotting to seize some tawdry advantage, and there's more than a hint that both are prostitutes. It's the nasty innuendo of all this rather than the explicit charge that makes it so offensive, the suggestion that the Jew is always cheap, unclean, ravenous, clutching. It has been excused as one of the common, unexamined prejudices of the time. And though that was surely the case, it doesn't remove the squalid odor emitted by such insinuations, then as well as now.

We find the same arrogance in pre-Nazi art. One of my favorite examples is a painting of 1912 by Ludwig Fahrenkrog titled "The Holy Hour." In it we see a well-formed young man standing naked in a meadow raising his arms to the purifying rays of the sun while behind him gasping in the grass on his stomach is the twisted, thin-shanked figure of a man destined to crawl the earth like a snake because of his base passions. We don't know for sure that Fahrenkrog intended the latter to be a Jew, but we do know that Nazi artists found the painting inspirational. In any case, it's clear that cultural purity conveys to the central figure every right to turn his back on the pathetic wretch behind him.

The most chilling depiction of cultural superiority I've encountered occurs in Henry James's novel *The Portrait of a Lady*. In it, the heroine Isabel Archer, a young idealist, is manipulated into marrying Gilbert Osmond, an expatriate American who has moved to Italy, developed exquisite taste, and surrounded himself with fine objects. On the surface Osmond is a companionable man, but as we get to know him we discover that his affability is dependent upon his being able to select, or shape, all the objects around him, and that in his mind the people in his orbit are just as much objects as pieces of China he may have purchased. At one point, he is discussing with one of Isabel's former suitors the joys of marriage, and he explains why it's pleasing to him:

> I delight, to this hour, in my wife's conversation. If you are ever bored, get married. Your wife indeed may bore you in that case; but you will never bore yourself. You will always have something to say to yourself—always have a subject of reflection.

In other words, a wife is an object that helps one to pass time in a diverting way. And this is the only function Osmond can imagine another person serving. He loves his daughter—from a previous union—as well as he can love anything, but he thinks of her as something to be shaped properly under his hand. He wants her to be aesthetically pleasing to him. He defends his decision to send her back to a convent school, after she has been allowed some freedom, in this way:

> The convent is a great institution; we can't do without it; it corresponds to an essential need in families, in society. It's a school of good manners; it's a school of repose. Oh, I don't want to detach my daughter from the world. I don't want to make her fix her thoughts on the other one. This one is very well, after all, and she may think of it as much as she chooses. Only she must think of it in the right way.

It doesn't take Isabel long to discover that she has married a monster, and only a bit longer to decide that the only way to save herself is to flee from him.

There are too many Gilbert Osmonds in the world, and they are encouraged by being praised as educated men. But, there's no education in them. Their learning has puffed them up whereas education has just the opposite effect. It teaches us our need to know the minds of other people so we can repair our own flaws and find joy in the well-being of others. If cultivation doesn't lead us in that direction, it's a sham.

Next time, I'll take up the third of my false, or confused, visions of education.

The notion that the goal of education is the production of experts may be the most noxious creed of our anti-educational faith.

*P*ERHAPS EVEN MORE harmful than ideas of the educated person as money-maker or cultural epigone is the notion of educated person as expert. Certainly, it has had a more deleterious effect on university life than anything else, and it has been the source of the most fatuous pronouncements I've ever heard.

When I was a student at the University of Puget Sound, the then famous historian Henry Steele Commager came to give a lecture. The history department held a luncheon for him in the faculty dining room and invited the senior history majors to attend. When we had finished eating, Commager was asked to make a few remarks, and he decided to comment on the practices required to make a good historian. One of the first things he said was that the serious student of history must read four books a day.

I looked round at the other members of the audience and saw them all nodding as though they had just been brushed by the owl of wisdom. I began to wonder if I had fallen in with a pack of idiots. Having been an engineering student, I was in the habit, when any quantitative matter was broached, of doing some quick figuring about its implications. Just a moment's mental arithmetic told me that four books a day over the course of a normal career would add up to sixty thousand books. It was a perfectly silly number deriving from a perfectly silly statement. Yet, there it was, receiving respect from a supposedly learned audience. It was one of the first occasions when I was shown that learnedness is no defense against selective derangement. There have been plenty of others since then.

When I was studying Victorian literature with Cecil Lang at the University of Virginia, I met with a similar breakdown. One day when he was talking about the problems of interpreting Tennyson, he said something to the effect that a major difficulty lay in the requirement of having to read all that had ever been written about Tennyson. The presumption was that this was required of a scholar before he could begin to do any serious work of his own. Consider it. Do you know how much has been written about Tennyson? And do you know what percentage of it is utter crap? Just think of the belief that one must wade through piles of garbage in order to have the right to comment on a great poet; one must spend a good portion of his life on nonsense before he can speak his own mind about words that are right in front of his face. It's an ideal fit only for cretins—and, perhaps, not even for them—and yet it was the ideal presented to me throughout my graduate study. "Success" was presumed to be dependent upon an apostolic laying on of hands by people whose beliefs were unexamined and wildly unrealistic. Such is graduate education in the humanities.

It's not as though the emptiness of the ideal hasn't been pointed out to us over and again. A principal theme of Emerson's great essay "The American Scholar" is the manner in which books are misused. As he says:

> Books are the best of things well used; abused, among the worst. What is the right use? What is the one end, which all means go to effect? They are for nothing but to inspire. I had better never see a book, than to be warped by its attraction clean out of my own orbit, and made a satellite instead of a system.

So what if you pack your head as full as you can pack it with information about some little thing, unless you use that information to bring forth your own thought? If the purpose of scholarship is to know everything written about Tennyson, why not just be a CD ROM instead of a human being? The theory holds, of course, that we prepare ourselves to think by seeing what others have thought. That would be fine if that were the way things actually worked in the schools. But when the cult of expertise takes over, having a thought is less important than being able to cite a source, and after a while, the notion that there should be a thought behind a flood of sources is forgotten. At an academic conference I attended last month the majority of papers were little more than piles of sources, one on top of the other, with scarcely any thought to be pulled out of them no matter how you racked your brain. And every one of these papers was presented by a "doctor of philosophy."

The hardest thing I had to do as a teacher was to convince students that education was something other than demonstrating to me what they had read. I have worked through thousands of student papers littered with useless references that had nothing to do with what was supposedly being said. When I would ask why they were there, I always got the same answer: "I thought I was supposed to show you what I know." When I would answer, "No, you're supposed to show me what you think, so we can have a conversation about it, and, maybe, make your thought stronger," I got the identical blank look.

My colleagues generally attributed this problem to student dullness and lack of imagination. But, I can't agree. I think it came about because that's what the students had been taught to do. And when I go to conferences and observe professors doing the same thing my students did, only with a bit more polish in citing sources, my suspicion is strengthened.

The origin of this source-mongering is envy. During the second half of the nineteenth century, when most of the "humanistic" disciplines were organized, physical science was making such great strides it promised to answer every question. Scholars who studied human affairs didn't want to miss out on the prestige conferred by "science," so they proposed to collect data in proportions that would allow the same degree of precision attained by physicists. The problem was that they were very bad at arithmetic. They failed to consider that when dealing with human motivation the total number of influences is so great the percentage one can factor into a system of analysis is statistically insignificant. Even when analysis chops the human being up into supposedly manageable components, such as "economic man," the problem does not go away. "Social science" has always been an oxymoron, and presumably always will be, unless we come on some method of collecting and analyzing data that now appears beyond possibility. This is not a new revelation. It has been pointed out ever since social science began the march of arrogance that perverted the purposes of the university. Leo Tolstoy, in the 1860s, noted that the moral, political, and spiritual worlds are permanently out of the realm of science. The proportion in them of submerged, uninspectable life is too high.

The great intellectual historian Isaiah Berlin describes the problem this way:

> We are part of a larger scheme of things than we can understand. We cannot describe it in the way in which external objects or the characters of other people can be described by isolating them somewhat from the historical "flow" in which they have their being, and from the "submerged," unfathomed portions of themselves to which professional historians have, according to Tolstoy, paid so little heed.

Just because collective human behavior cannot be scientifically analyzed doesn't mean that it can't be studied, or that nothing can be learned about it. But the process of learning in fields dealing with people (or at least fields involving human volition) is different from that in fields dealing with protons. In the latter, we employ methodical inquiry, whereas in human studies we try to develop a sense of reality which permits estimates of the likelihood of certain occurrences. And, our powers of estimation grow the more we look out into the world and engage in honest and attentive discourse. By this practice we develop beliefs about what is of greater, or lesser, importance, what counts and what doesn't count, what lasts and what will quickly pass away. We begin to see the things in front of us as symbols of things we can't see, and we learn that some symbols have more power than others.

In my newspaper yesterday, there was a photograph of Ben Cohen and Jerry Greenfield, the founders of Ben and Jerry's, standing with Richard Goldstein, the CEO of Unilever, the corporation that has recently taken over the ice cream company. Mr. Goldstein's hair is carefully coifed; it's hard to tell when either Ben or Jerry might have had a haircut. Mr. Goldstein is wearing a tie that probably cost well over a hundred dollars; there is no sign of a tie on either Ben or Jerry. Mr. Goldstein's shirt is lavender, with white collar and cuffs, the latter fastened by cufflinks; both Ben and Jerry are wearing rumpled short-sleeved shirts of indistinct character. All three are smiling, but even here the similarity is more forced than real. The smiles from Ben and Jerry are what you might see any day in the local coffee shop; Mr. Goldstein's smile is controlled. His mouth is not open whereas we can see both Ben's and Jerry's teeth shining forth.

For a person who knows anything about the economic culture of modern America, the picture is full of meaning. It says entrepreneurs versus manager, socially concerned men versus money-concerned man, men who care nothing for fashion versus man who is obsessed with fashion, men who don't conceal their thoughts versus a man who would never reveal his thoughts. Yet, here's the kicker: this could all be wrong. So far as the picture serves as evidence, Mr. Goldstein might be warm, generous, socially active, and Ben and Jerry might be the most mean-spirited money grubbers you would ever want to come across. The symbolism of the picture allows us to make an estimate, but it doesn't allow us to be sure. This is the nature of what might be called philosophic knowledge, knowledge that we derive from our sense of reality. It points us in certain directions, it raises certain prospects in our minds, it gives us possibilities we may need to investigate further. It does not ever give a final answer, and it prods us always to want to learn more. Knowledge of this kind is the primary goal of education.

As we move from knowledge that can be scientifically derived to knowledge that's derived from a sense of reality, we can rely less and less on expertise. If a guy really knows how a Ford engine works, and he tells you honestly what's wrong with it, you have good reason to believe him. But, if a guy tells you that your conclusions about a personal problem are coming from a psychological "disorder," then you can take it into account, but your reason for believing him is much less strong. Our principal educational problem nowadays is that we have come to believe there are far more experts than actually exist. As historian Roger Hausheer puts it, "the overwhelming majority is today uncritically in thrall to more or less crude forms of scientism." Or, we can go back to Isaiah Berlin, who tells us, " the absolute authority of a secular priesthood has been realized only too successfully in our day."

There is no more important function for education than freeing ourselves from the authority of a secular priesthood of experts. Obviously, we don't, as educated people, free ourselves from that priesthood if we assume that education itself is a ticket into it. Education has to be something different, something critical of, something that tempers expertise, if it's going to serve liberation.

This completes my ruminations on things education is commonly thought to be, but isn't. I might have done similar treatments of professional standing, credentialism, or even intellectualism. But as I said earlier, three examples are enough to show what can be done with others. Now, I'll go on to a series of dialogues with persons who have achieved notable success doing what I'm trying to do more humbly in these letters. I want to look at them with a view to discovering what we can still celebrate in their beliefs, and what, in light of modern conditions, we might want to modify. I'll start with a genuinely wonderful book, John Henry Newman's *Idea of a University*.

Until next time.

*Here I began a series of six letters to show that powerful think-
ers over the past century and a half have found the educational
theories of the degree salesmen and the modern professoriate as
lacking as I do. I reasoned that if bright people over that length
of time perceive a similar problem, there must be something real
about it.*

NEWMAN'S *Idea of a University* is a very great book. I'm not sure it's
coherent, but its lack of coherence may be a principal feature of its greatness. It's fractured by a division between what it says is good in this world
and what is good eternally. Newman labors mightily to show how these two
goods interact, but I don't think he ever fully explains their connection,
and, maybe, considering his sense of ultimate virtue, it's impossible to weave
them perfectly together.

When we take up a book from the 1850s we need to remember that there
was a powerful force at work in the Western world which nowadays, though
still present for some, is not nearly as powerful. I'm speaking of the concept
of salvation. It's a wonderful idea, for all its intellectual limitations. God
has prepared a great good place for us which can be ours eternally if we will
use this life on earth as God means us to use it. We don't have to worry
about where this place is or about the nature of its reality. God will take
care of all that, and it will all be revealed to us in good time. What we must
do in the meantime is to live, think, behave, and believe as we have been
instructed to do. The kicker is that these instructions are often hard to
square with ordinary notions of getting on well in the world. Still, considering the ratio between eternity and any finite length of time, the world's
notions of well-being don't count for much.

Newman held a potent belief in salvation, potent because it wasn't for him, as it has been for most Christians, a passive assent but rather the driving passion of his existence. Since he was a person who possessed what Dwight Culler has called an "imperial intellect," he reasoned that God would not have created this place of perfection without also providing a guide for getting to it. What's the sense of having a place if we don't also have a means of reaching it? For Newman, God was not a being who would violate the canons of good sense.

When Newman surveyed human history he saw only one reasonable candidate for this necessary guide, and that was the Holy Catholic Church. Therefore, in midlife, in what was probably the most famous conversion of history, he left the Church of England and went over to the Church of Rome. From that time forward, the Catholic Church became for him the final tribunal for resolving all issues of authority on earth. If it is indeed God's agent on earth, God being God, that makes perfect sense. Newman tried with all his might to remain faithful to that sense for the rest of his days.

We have to remember this, though: just because a guy changes churches, and stops wearing suits and starts wearing long black dresses, he doesn't get a new brain. All Newman knew, all he recalled, was still lodged in that brain. He might now have a new perspective, but he still carried with him the thoughts, habits, and attitudes of a finely educated English gentleman. It was these, I think, which had as large an influence on the varied writings that were finally collected as *Idea of a University* as his undoubted devotion to the Church. The churchly influences were powerful but the passionate language of the book seems usually to come from Newman's ideal of how gentlemen should behave themselves toward one another. He was, I suspect, a thinker somewhat at odds with himself, though he had such a facility with rhetoric that it's not easy to discover the division. Education he saw as the process by which men become gentlemen in their dealings with one another and with the world. Here is his definition of what we should seek from a university education: "the force, the steadiness, the comprehensiveness and the versatility of intellect, the command over our own powers, the instinctive just estimate of things as they pass before us." It's as though he had Jane Austen's Mr. Knightley in mind as he wrote the sentence (as well he might have, for he was a great reader of Jane Austen).

We come into the possession of these things—force, steadiness, versatile intellect, and just estimation—by developing habits of mind which flow from the practice of the liberal arts, and these habits are freedom, equitableness, calmness, moderation, and wisdom. And for Newman, the main purpose of a university is to induce these habits of mind in its students. A university may have other purposes, of course: professional training, the advancement of knowledge, development of the practical arts and sciences. But unless helping students towards educated habits of mind is the first purpose, then an institution has no right to the name of university.

When I said in the first letters of this series that the university should put education at its center and should resist with all its power the attempts of the degree salesmen to drive it out into the wilderness, I was saying no more than Newman is saying here. It's well for both of us to say this, and I think it's morally true. Yet, it doesn't amount to a hill of beans unless we can each make the case that there is a causal relationship between the activities we support and the habits of mind we admire.

Newman has ostensibly made his case for a great many readers. His book is a classic, and one expects to see it mentioned whenever any discussion of educational ideals is introduced. Still, I wonder how many of those who cite Newman have actually read him, or have made the imaginative effort to penetrate his elegant style to see exactly what he was saying. It's possible to read him in a blah-blah sort of way, nodding the head in agreement because the words sound nice. It's possible to agree with him in the same way the new president expects agreement when he says we all want the same things but have some differences about how to get them. But just as I certainly don't want the same things George Bush wants, I don't want to agree with Newman because he can string together a fine-sounding set of attributes and call them the qualities of an educated mind. I want, instead, to know exactly where I do agree with him and where I may find myself out of his orbit.

Since my purpose here is not to offer a critique of Newman but rather enter into a kind of dialogue with him in order to clarify my own thought, I need to introduce those components of his thinking that strike me as a bit skewed so far as education is concerned. But before I move into an explanation of our differences I have a duty to pay him tribute as one of my first teachers on the subject of liberal education and as a writer I continue to admire. Newman, in my estimation, had a wonderful mind, sharp, clear, elegant. But if, in these later ages, it's permissible to distinguish mind from psyche, I'm forced to conclude that his psychological constitution lacked the winning power of his mind.

A feature of Newman's life which most of his biographers have emphasized—generally with approval—is, as he called it, a visitation by deep imagination in the fall of 1816, which took hold of him and told him that it was God's will that he should lead a single life, that God had work for him to do that would require this sacrifice. His heart was captured, as one of his biographers put it, by "the Christian ideal of holiness." Newman was fifteen years old at the time.

I am not such a devotee of modern sensibilities to say, as many of my acquaintances would, that the boy was in need of counselling. But I do suspect that he needed intellectual companionship of a kind he did not get, and in the loneliness of his grand romantic heart he seized on an ideal that had too much of convention and not enough of originality. That Christian holiness has been associated with rejection of the flesh is the single most unfortunate feature of a great religion, one with which we continue to struggle and probably will have to struggle for generations to come. It would take a far more powerful historian than I can hope to be to figure out how purity came to be identified with sensual innocence, but it's clear that the identity was firmly in place when Newman was born and that it bedeviled his generation more than any other concept. In truth, it drove many of his compatriots insane.

What has this to do with education one might ask. I would answer, not everything, but a great deal. Education is involved with leading one to the goods of life, and if in someone's thought one of life's inevitabilities is seen not as a blessing, but as its opposite, his vision of education is bound to be affected. Over and again, I find myself in reading Newman saying, "Yes! and yes! and yes!" and then, suddenly, being brought up by the thought, "Wait; something's missing here."

Newman's blind spot is hidden within his analysis of nature, which in many respects is compelling. He sees that education must be an overcoming of nature, that the natural man is, essentially, the thoughtless man, the man who does not know how to bring patterns out of the welter of stimuli perpetually flooding his senses. For the natural man everything is vaguely "there" and nothing is precisely there. In perhaps the most acute passage of his book, Newman makes the following point:

> It is this haziness of intellectual vision which is the malady of all classes of men by nature, of those who read and write and compose, quite as well as those who cannot,—of all who have not had a really good education. Those who cannot either read or write may, nevertheless, be in the number of those who have remedied and got rid of it; those who can are too often still under its power. It is an acquisition quite separate from miscellaneous information, or knowledge of books.

No writer I know is stronger than Newman in discriminating between schooling and education. In that respect he stands as one of the finest anti-degree salesmen in the English tradition. He is able to take this stand because he sees knowledge as a whole and not as a jumble of fragments to be packaged up and sold. He was modern enough to perceive that danger even in the middle of the nineteenth century. As he said of the degree salesmen of his day, "They argue as if every thing, as well as every person, had its price." And when people approach knowledge in that frame of mind they leave the university "so shallow as not even to know their own shallowness."

In all this Newman's perception was as clear as anyone's can be. Yet, because he took the Church as God's oracle on earth, he set it and its teachings in place of a faculty that I think stands at the core of the educational impulse. It wouldn't be right to say that Newman dismisses imagination, but he does discount it, and particularly that portion of it that issues from the sensual drives. He doesn't flinch from the truth that we must direct our sight to all that is human. His analysis of the fundamental organization of knowledge is one the modern university would do well to adopt.

> There are three great subjects on which Human Reason employs itself: God, Nature, and Man: and theology being put aside in the present argument, the physical and social worlds remain. These, when respectively subjected to Human Reason, form two books: the book of nature is called Science, the book of man is called Literature. Literature and Science thus considered nearly constitute the subject matter of Liberal Education.

Still, having paid this tribute to literature, he then goes on to say that it is necessarily corrupt because it is the expression of man's sin. And this is true of it regardless of its source: "on the whole all literatures are one; they are the voices of the natural man." Whenever the concept of natural man arises, we find Newman circling back to his horror of the flesh, or, as he puts it, "the inconceivable evil of sensuality." His style, usually cool and elegant, takes on a different tone when he confronts the presence of sensual behavior, as in this passage on the character of a people's literature:

> National Literature is, in a parallel way, the untutored movements of the reason, imagination, passions, and affections of the natural man, the leapings and the friskings, the plunging and the snortings, the sportings and the buffoonings, the clumsy play and the aimless toil, of the noble, lawless savage of God's intellectual creation.

Plunging, snorting, sporting, and buffooning are not exactly the habits we associate with John Henry Newman, and that he chose language of this kind to speak of men's natural inclinations shows that he had little intellectual sympathy for the idea that they might constitute an element of human meaning, and, even, a kind of salvation. We can't chide him because he was not Nietzsche or D. H. Lawrence, and yet it's not unreasonable to assume that he could have been an even greater man than he was had he not been in thrall to a chilly asceticism.

One doesn't have to be a sexual athlete to believe that bodily pleasures can lead to interactions that rise above themselves. It is good for people to eat together, and play together, and, yes, touch one another in ways that set nerves atingle. Out of all that comes a discourse that helps us to know ourselves, and know other people, and understand our duties one to the other. If I had to choose between a friend who would sit with me, drink a bottle of wine, and tell me honestly what he is about, on the one hand, and a church that would continually set me straight, on the other, there's no doubt which I would pick. Maybe the difference between me and Newman is simply a matter of separate historical eras. In any event, it is not right to emphasize mightily differences with a thinker one can in most instances support. Newman was a serious man, and to read him in a time when it's hard to imagine encountering a serious person in a public place is an experience of breath-taking sweetness. I love his words and so I have to love the soul that brought them forth, though I admit that were I to be projected back in time and meet the flesh and blood man, I might find his personality a hard crust to crack.

I'm now going to take a few days off from letter writing to celebrate the holidays. When I start back in the new year, I'll continue with the dialogues I initiated here, and probably turn my attention to Ralph Waldo Emerson and his ideal of an American scholar. Still, remember, these are letters, and they are written in the midst of actual experiences. So if someone else forces himself on my attention I may get diverted from Emerson. In any case, I'll send another mailing about the fifth of January—which really will be the new millennium.

Happy holidays.

We have among the American muses a voice that makes my criticisms of the academy sound like elevator music. Whenever I find my courage faltering because what I see in front of me seems too flaccid to be real, I return to Emerson to remind myself of how very timid I am.

*T*HE CURIOUS THING about Emerson's essay "The American Scholar" is how it comes to be so often cited and anthologized. It's scarcely complimentary to the tribe of citers and anthologizers. If you think I've been critical of the degree salesmen, you should take a look at them through Emerson's eyes. Before you do, though, beware. It's depressing to view modern university practices in the light of Emerson's ideal.

"The American Scholar" was first delivered as an address to the Phi Beta Kappa Society of Cambridge on August 31, 1837. A few days earlier, in his journal, Emerson had written:

> The hope to arouse young men at Cambridge to a worthier view of their literary duties prompts me to offer the theory of the Scholar's function. He has an office to perform in society. What is it? To arouse the intellect; to keep it erect & sound; to keep admiration in the hearts of the people; to keep the eye open upon its spiritual aims.

With those four duties in mind, you can see how degraded the concept of scholar has become, though to be fair, we have to admit that even in the nineteenth century it was already far below the ideal. Emerson's vision of "scholar" was that of "man thinking" and applying his thought to the issues of life—the real issues rather than the trivialities that commonly agitate the academy.

The mind of the race in America, Emerson said, had taken another direction, towards property. Just imagine his watching an evening of modern television. He would be on his knees praying to be transported back to the corruptions of his own time. Yet, even then "young men of fairest promise, inflated by the mountain winds, shined upon by all the stars of God, find the earth below not in unison with these,—but are hindered from action by the disgust which the principles on which business is managed inspire."

If we can believe Emerson, at least the young men then knew enough to be disgusted. Nowadays the saddest thing about the university is the squandering of money, time, effort, life, on shoddy goods students have been propagandized into accepting. They graduate, proud of their degrees, not knowing they've been flim-flammed. I talked just last week with a young graduate who could speak intelligently about nothing other than the forty thousand dollars a year she was sure her degree was going to command. I suppose her teachers are satisfied with the work they did with her. After all, she paid money for it, didn't she?

The difference between the way we use the word "scholar" and the way Emerson used it is so complete I suspect most students who are assigned the essay have trouble understanding what it's about. Nothing in their university experience is likely to have prepared them for anything as radical as Emerson's thought. When he says that a fatal disservice is done if one mind receives its truth from another, he is speaking of an individualism so thoroughgoing no institution could fully promote it. Institutions seek to make use of people and Emerson wanted people who could make use of institutions. I'm with him in that, but I wonder if the methods Emerson propounded can still fully command our faith.

If I had had the energy to become a scholar myself, I suspect the subject I would have taken up would have been the concept of "nature" in the nineteenth century. It was an idea so prepossessing, so powerful, so comprehensive, so self-evident that it far surpasses anything people can give themselves to today. Emerson says that nature is the first influence upon the mind: first in importance, first in everything. It's hard to know exactly what he meant when he said things like that, but he implies that the reality in which we are immersed is sending us signals about our individual purposes, and that if we will simply open ourselves to them, we will be led on to the sure ground and meaning of life.

Emerson could talk this way because he believed that nature was charged with humanistic values, or, to be more accurate, that human values and nature both derive from the same unifying spirit. As he said, "this ethical character so penetrates the bone and marrow of nature, as to seem the end for which it was made." And, then, just a little farther on: "The moral law lies at the center of nature and radiates to the circumference."

But does it? Does nature have a moral law that can offer genuine solace to humans? These are philosophical questions that reach beyond my scope here. I bring them up not to answer them, but just to point out that the nineteenth century still believed in some kind of thing "out there" in which we could find our help, whereas we, having passed through the horrors of the twentieth century, no longer feel so sure about the something outside ourselves that will guide us down the right path. It's not that we can't still find the same beauty in nature that Emerson hymned so eloquently in his great essay of that name. I, for example, in writing this felt my mind go stale, and so I put Emerson to the test. I went out and shoveled snow for an hour. It worked after a fashion. I was able to return to my chair in a better frame of mind than when I left it. But I don't know if that was because nature offered me spiritual beauty or because my blood was circulating more vigorously. Maybe those are the same things. At any rate, nature is more an enigma to me than it was to Emerson.

I wander off my track. I'm not here to analyze Emerson's views of nature, but rather to use him to help me think about education. And what he tells me on that score is that education involves consulting something that is not grounded in social egotism. Whether it's nature or something else, it has to exist if education is to be possible, because the social conventions just won't do. They lead us to captivity and not to independence, which is the goal of the educated mind. On this point Emerson couldn't be more clear: "In self-trust all the virtues are comprehended. Free should the scholar be,—free and brave." And why does he have to be brave? Because he has to accept "the state of virtual hostility in which he seems to stand to society, and especially to educated society" (Emerson is using "educated" here as I have been using "schooled"). I'm happy to read sentiments like these because they tell me that my own revulsion from the degree salesmen is not merely eccentric, that others have felt it, and, in many cases more strongly than I. They are the voices who start us towards education. I might digress here to say that one of the first things that struck me when I started to college was that my real teachers, Jane Austen, and Charles Dickens, and Samuel Johnson, for example, were offering lessons almost directly opposite to the lessons offered by the figures the authorities had chosen to stick in the front of the classroom. "Why should this be so?" I would ask in my sophomoric ignorance. And then I would go on to wonder which of the two I should pick if I were forced to pick one of them.

What this something from which we can learn might be, for us, I hope to make clearer as I go along. But, I've already been hinting at it by talking about genuine discourse and all the complexities it involves. Emerson suggests the true nature of discourse when he says, "A great soul will be strong to live as well as strong to think." The great teachers down the ages tell us the same thing: when thought is good thought it will lead to good action. And this, in turn, suggests something about the degree salesmen and their ally, the common professor.

The hardest component of this subject to convey, because it is so perfectly taken for granted, is the psychological power of professordom. Professors themselves cannot imagine the control being exercised over them because they do not envision the prospect of thinking as men and women. They think, mainly, as professors, which, in truth, is scarcely to think at all. It would be more accurate to designate their mental activity as scheming. And scheming is not an educative activity.

What is it that men and women do? They eat, and sleep, and talk with their friends about what they have been able to learn from experience, and walk in the woods, and wonder about life, and hope to find expressible rewards for their children. What do professors do? They go to committee meetings, and strive for tenure, and hustle book contracts, and try to get speaking engagements, and denounce administrators for not making enough travel money available to them. We can say all we wish that these are simply two strains of a unified life. But, that's a lie. They are separate categories of being, and education applies only to one of them. It's meaningless to speak of educating a professor. The only objects of education are men and women.

We should recur continually to that very famous passage near the beginning of "The American Scholar":

> But, unfortunately, this original unit, this fountain of power, has been so distributed to multitudes, has been so minutely subdivided and peddled out, that it is spilled into drops and cannot be gathered. The state of society is one in which the members have suffered amputation from the trunk, and strut about so many walking monsters— a good finger, a neck, a stomach, an elbow, but never a man.

It is fine to have a good elbow so long as it is attached to a person. It is fine to be a professor, so long as the professordom is a subordinate feature of an educated man or woman. But let the professor take the lead, let the book contract count for more than conversation with colleagues and students, and then we have the strutting monster of Emerson's metaphor, a person who is taking the same stance towards life as the degree salesmen take towards education. And, when the part leads the whole, all becomes stale.

Most professors use books not as a supplement to life but as a retreat from life. They think from books in order not to have to think from life. Doing the latter would force them to act, and what professors want above all else is to avoid the dangers of action. This is why, despite the piddly noises of opposition they sometimes make, they won't actually challenge the degree salesmen. It is more comfortable to be their fellow travelers.

Even so, we can take hope from the curious fact with which I began. The professors themselves occasionally recommend Emerson. They recommend a voice which tells them they are, in their everyday pursuits, fools. What does this mean? It means, I hope, that the longing for education, however misguided one's actual practices have become, persists. It means that some portion of the self desires the quality which Emerson says all mature men and women come to prize: "We learn to prefer imperfect theories, and sentences, which contain glimpses of truth, to digested systems which have no one valuable suggestion."

I suspect Emerson will continue to be read, at least by a few, for the message that men and women thinking are more alive, and more educated, than dealers in digested systems.

In writing these letters nothing has vexed me more than deciding who should be the subjects of these dialogues. The number of prospects is uncountable. Yet, I've chosen to limit myself to a half-dozen. So, how can I pick the best six out of all I might pick? Obviously, I can't. The six I choose won't be the best six. They'll be simply six thinkers who have presented themselves to me insistently because of qualities in their thought that have spoken to my own experiences. A great charade of intellectual life is the notion that one selects evidence in accord with rational, objective principles. It's not so. The voices we choose to bring forward are, in a sense, reflections of self. But since they do belong to other persons, in other times and places, they suggest that we are not entirely solipsistic.

With that in mind, I'll go on next time to Matthew Arnold, the third of my six.

To relate the thought of Matthew Arnold to the intellectual condition of modern American college athletes is, perhaps, not a task a sane man would attempt. Yet, it seems to me that Arnold, in a general way, was prophetic about the conditions that brought the jock mentality to its current elevated status.

A RECENT NUMBER of *The New Yorker* has a review which fits perfectly with thoughts Matthew Arnold suggests to me, but does it with up-to-date information which Arnold, having been dead for more than a century, can't quite manage. The review is by sociologist Louis Menand, and the book is *The Game of Life,* by James L. Shulman and William G. Bowen. It's a heavily statistical portrait of the college athletes enrolled in thirty-two fairly selective institutions which have been studied over the past fifty years by the Andrew W. Mellon Foundation.

The findings are reputed to be surprising. It is not just in the big name athletic powerhouses like Michigan and Florida State that athletes are coddled and allowed to escape normal academic expectations. In truth, this happens on a larger scale in academically prestigious places like Swarthmore, Williams, and Stanford. The reason is that in the toney places, a greater percentage of students participate in varsity athletics. In 1997-98, for example, the University of Michigan had six hundred and sixty-six varsity athletes enrolled. Williams had seven hundred and fifteen. Yet, the University of Michigan has more than ten times the number of students Williams does.

One might think that in the supposedly higher quality institutions the athletes come closer to the academic norm than do the athletes that play before national television cameras on Saturday afternoons. That was, indeed, the case fifty years ago. But, no longer. In all the institutions studied, the athletes do far worse than the norm and worse even than was predicted by their entering SAT scores, which are already well below those of their non-athletic classmates.

Data of this sort in the minds of conventional thinkers point to the progressive corruption of academics by athletics. But conventional thinkers are conventional because they see only the surface of things. They have small aptitude for probing into the genuine causes of observed phenomena. Louis Menand stays mostly on the border of conventionality, but he does have the ability sometimes to peek over the line. To a degree he accepts the conclusions of Shulman and Bowen, who believe that mania over the virtues of competition drives the athletic craze. But, occasionally, he digs deeper and suggests avenues of speculation more interesting than the authors can manage. Late in his review, for example, he says:

> What's fascinating about "The Game of Life," though, isn't the shadow it casts on college sports. It's the light it sheds, almost inadvertently, on college in general. Nearly everything Shulman and Bowen say about students who are athletes has implications for the way we think about students who are not. Many people believe, for example, that athletic virtues translate into social virtues. Shulman and Bowen are fairly certain that the main thing athletes carry off the playing field and into life after college is the belief that competition is good, which as they point out, is not the belief a liberal arts education was meant to inculcate.

When we get to the belief the liberal arts are supposed to produce, we are approaching something interesting. It's at that point though that Menand and almost all modern speculators fail us because they don't view education as an essential ingredient of social purpose. I don't want to misrepresent them. They do see schooling as a necessary part of social functioning. Yet education in its purity is perceived almost as icing on the cake: something nice but not a thing we need fundamentally to worry about. To find education treated as it should be, we have to go to greater thinkers than any now before us, or at least any that have managed to achieve a public reputation. To my mind, Matthew Arnold fits that description, though you'd scarcely know it from the way Arnold has been discussed by late twentieth century scholars and critics.

Arnold's reputation is a good example of the evils of departmentalism. Because he has been pigeon-holed as a literary figure, he is written about mostly by professors of English. It would be hard to find a group less prescient about the great social problems facing us than the current tribe that teaches literature in American colleges and universities. They can't take the measure of Arnold as a social critic because they have little grasp of the forces and attitudes that make society what it is. They are a self-obsessed coterie, and the notion that their subject, literature, belongs to all people and should play a significant role in the everyday life of all people, is outside their imagination. Since Arnold did understand that literature is an essential ingredient of civilized life, they tend to write him off either as a naive idealist, or, more commonly, as an intellectual snob.

Arnold was neither. No one had a more practical grasp of the educational problems of his time. And because he had a good mind he thought about the problems of his own era in the light of the educational challenges of all times.

In 1858, the British government appointed a royal commission to look into the question of how society could offer "sound and cheap elementary instruction to all classes of people." Officials called assistant commissioners were sent out to survey current activities throughout Britain, and, in addition, two assistant commissioners were selected to visit European countries and report on practices there. Arnold was chosen as one of the latter, with responsibility for France and Holland. After extensive travels and visiting, Arnold filed his report with the commission and then asked for permission to publish it separately. Permission was granted, and on May 4, 1861, his book called *The Popular Education of France* appeared in the bookshops. The book was almost identical to the report, with one exception. Since the book was appearing on its own, Arnold felt it needed an introduction, and consequently he wrote an essay of about thirty pages titled "Democracy" to serve that purpose. The introduction turned out to have a more robust life than the book itself, and, in time, came to be seen as one of the nineteenth century's signal statements of educational and political philosophy.

Arnold excels current commentators by understanding that education and politics are different facets of the same thing, a thing we don't have a common name for in contemporary discourse but which nonetheless remains a unity despite our inability to see it as one. I'm not a good maker-up of names and can't find a better title for it than the national spirit, a term easily misinterpreted. The truth remains, though, that every people has a best self, a self that its most acute thinkers would want it to be known for down the ages. If we can call this self the national spirit, then we can understand that education is the way we discover and expand it and that politics is the manner in which we apply it to the problems of ordinary living. We can also see that if education doesn't discover it, then politics is crippled in applying it. That's what's going on in America now. Education has failed to discover the best self of the American people and, therefore, politics is running sour.

In "Democracy," Arnold sliced to the core of the educational question by asking who or what was going to supply the ideal of "high reason and right feeling" that would guide the English nation towards its best self. That's a question educated people must always have before them: what provides the ideal, and what keeps it fresh and compatible with new conditions? It's a question the American people don't begin to have an answer for at the moment.

Arnold explained that until the middle part of the nineteenth century, the English aristocracy—an aristocracy of birth and land-holding—had provided an ideal, and had done so pretty well. It had been, perhaps, the most successful aristocracy of history. But an aristocracy is notoriously incapable of dealing with ideas. And in a period of rapid change of the sort

Western populations were facing in the mid-nineteenth century, the power of ideas became the life of the people. So, the issue was, what could shape those ideas into a "grandeur of spirit?" What could keep them from becoming "lowered or dulled"? Then, to clinch his point, Arnold asked the critical question: what influence could be found to prevent the English people from becoming Americanized?

It wasn't a query that won him immense popularity on this side of the water. But, here, one hundred and forty years later, it's a question we ought to be mature enough to appreciate. Arnold saw America as a place where the multitude was in power with no adequate ideal to elevate or guide it. The middle class in England was coming dangerously close to emulating America because it had only two ideas: belief in liberty and belief in industry. These were certainly energizing beliefs, as America had shown. Yet, by themselves they were inadequate to fashion a humane culture. They created, Arnold said, character without culture, which is always raw, blind, and dangerous.

Before we dismiss Arnold as an English snob, perhaps we ought to listen to the words of the mayor of Chicago, reported in the *Chicago Sun Times* just a few weeks ago:

> If Chicago is going to continue to attract and retain high-tech companies, our schools have to produce graduates with the skills these companies require. The idea is not to listen to those who run education but to listen to the employers. What do they require?

If that's not a raw, blind, and dangerous statement, then it's not possible to make one. Yet, it's echoed by politicians throughout the nation, over and over again. It's fairly well in line with the spirit of "educational" reform being pushed by the new president, a reform too vague and tenuous to have much effect, but which, to the degree it takes a stance, defines education simply as technical proficiency, to be measured by tests which are neither accurate nor valid.

What, indeed, do the employers require? What does Richard M. Daley think they require? Are these requirements good for the spirit of the nation? What sort of national self will they bring forth? Will it be our best self? To list such questions is to realize how impossible it would be to have them asked in a public forum. The questions that most need answering are the questions that are now impermissible to ask, which is a curious situation in a nation presumed to be focused on education.

Arnold's answer to the larger question, a question I honor him for asking, may have been a sensible solution for his time. But it isn't an answer we can any longer fully embrace. For him, the only replacement for the values of the aristocracy, an aristocracy swamped by a sea of new ideas it couldn't start to assimilate, was state action. He quoted Burke to the effect that the state is the nation in its collective and corporate character, and from that definition assumed that only the state had the resources to bring culture to the middle classes, which would soon be the ruling classes. We need to recollect, though, that Arnold wrote at a time when people possessed a more coherent vision of education than we do, one that was firmly grounded in knowledge of the best that had been written and thought. In America, we have been trying for at least three-quarters of a century to effect the solution Arnold advocated in the mid-nineteenth century. Our state-directed schools have not failed us completely but neither have they supplied the thrust towards high reason and right feeling a great national culture demands. They may have served the latter better than the former, but one thing we should have learned from our TV culture is that supposedly right feeling cut off from reason and knowledge is a fairly pathetic thing, and not a force to stand against a rapacious plutocracy. One of our disadvantages, compared with Arnold's England, is that we have no aristocracy, not even a stupid one. By contrast, our plutocracy, which creates aspirations for our youth in order to sell to them, is, with the possible exception of the criminal underworld, the most vulgar class in the nation.

I can't answer Arnold's larger question in a few sentences. That, in effect, is what this entire series is attempting and if, when I've finished, I've made even a start I'll count myself reasonably successful. I can, though, at this point, raise reservations about an answer some might offer. And that will bring me back to where I started, to the data supplied by the Mellon Foundation.

If we can't derive an ideal from a non-existent aristocracy, or from a state led by men who are themselves meanly educated, or from an educational bureaucracy wallowing in bad theory and inept management, where might it come from? We have no church, no religion, and the truth that the nation is littered with squabbling sects doesn't make up for them. There is only one other institutional source that might feasibly be seen as the progenitor of a national ideal, and that is our network of colleges and universities. They were once at the core of a touching faith. Myriads of parents sacrificed their own pleasures so their children might go to the university and be lifted to something finer than they had known. And if the parents weren't articulate enough to define it precisely, that doesn't obviate the truth that they saw it as something more important than the chance to get high paying employment. That naive faith has largely disappeared. The universities are securely integrated into the economic machine. They serve it, and the men who manage them view them essentially as economic units.

The result is the kind of reports we get from the Mellon Foundation data. Is it any wonder that the students turn towards athletics and regard academics simply as an annoyance that must be accommodated? Unless they, themselves, see an academic field as their professional grazing ground, why should they take it seriously? Scarcely anyone is telling them that literature, history, philosophy, religious thought, political theory are the means for lifting and transforming not only their own lives but the world around them. No one is telling them that without serious conversation on these topics life cannot proceed decently. The so-called liberal arts, as they are generally treated through the breadth of the American university system, are inferior to athletics. Coaches offer more than English professors do. The students aren't idiots. They see this and so they turn to the coaches, even though the consequence is shallow social thinking and a fairly noxious politics (Shulman and Bowen report that "college athletes today are more likely than their classmates to identify themselves as conservative, and to name being 'very well off financially' as an 'essential' or 'very important' goal in life.").

Just last week, Frank Luntz, the leading Republican pollster, informed us that "The people aren't looking for a Shakespeare. They'd rather have Ward Cleaver." The presumption is they'd also rather have Ward Cleaver than Jefferson or Lincoln, both of whom knew considerably more of Shakespeare than the current president does. If this is who we've become it's probably true that education has little chance among us and we had best turn ourselves over to the degree salesmen to be trained for corporate treadmills.

I doubt, though, that the people have honestly faced what that would mean. Some have it in mind that it would mean comfort. It would certainly mean the death of anything resembling democracy. The problem with democracy is that it's not a stable condition. As Arnold noted, "the danger for democracy is how to find and keep high ideals." And this is truly a danger because without high ideals democracy can't prevail. I'm optimistic enough (maybe childishly so) to believe that we're not really ready to abandon democratic ideals and that, as Matthew Arnold argued persistently, we need education to keep them alive.

Next time I'll go on to another democratic theorist, and the voice most closely associated with education in American thought: John Dewey.

In American intellectual history, the man most associated with educational thought is also a man connected to thought he never promoted. The reasons for the distortion of his reputation overlap with the reason a false notion of education pervades the schools.

*W*HEN WE COME to John Dewey, we encounter one of the strangest reputations in the history of thought. I know of no thinker who has been as misunderstood as Dewey has, and, in particular, no one who has been as misunderstood by his own disciples. The Deweyites have misread Dewey so badly as almost to have stood him on his head. Why they should have done this and how much responsibility Dewey himself bears for it are ongoing questions for American intellectual history.

I'm not going to answer them completely here. But to bring Dewey's ideas into relation with my own argument I have to hint at a few of the reasons for the distortion. The first, and most notorious, is literary style. Though Dewey has been called obscure that's not the problem. In fact, his writing is generally clear. One would have to be a bad reader not to get what he's saying. Yet, along with his clarity goes tediousness. His books are hard to get through because sleepiness intervenes, or the slightest distraction directs attention elsewhere. Dewey's works offer confirmation of a comment Dr. Johnson made about a Matthew Prior poem:

> Tediousness is the most fatal of all faults; negligence or errors are single, but tediousness pervades the whole: other faults are censured and forgotten, but the power of tediousness propagates itself.

The evil in Dewey's case has been that his style has caused him to be more talked about than read. As you know, I used to work at a college which was reputed to be grounded in Dewey's educational philosophy. A frustration for me there was that I found no one who had read Dewey's books. The most avid Deweyites on campus were people who got their Dewey second-hand, through interpreters. And I gradually came to see that the interpreters weren't a lot more knowledgeable than my colleagues were. I can't be sure how general the condition is among those who say they admire Dewey, but it clearly afflicts many of them. And it serves to remind us that empty abstraction is the bane of academic talk.

It's easier to say that you're an advocate for reconstructing education, to profess devotion to student-centered teaching, to proclaim the superiority of process over product (all progressive shibboleths) than it is to grind through Dewey's ponderous writings. But if you do, you find he was con-temptuous of many of the ideas put forward in his name. For example, as his biographer Alan Ryan has noted, Dewey wasn't student-centered; he was teacher-centered. The problem with his practical educational reforms was he had such a high ideal for what teachers should be able to do that you probably couldn't find a hundred people in the country, willing to teach little kids, who could meet his standards. When Dewey said that children should learn chemistry by processing grain and baking bread, he actually meant that they should learn chemistry. In the watered-down version of that preachment, which has been common among progressive teachers, making bread has been seen as more important than knowing chemistry. Obviously, it's simpler to mix, and puddle, and pop in the oven than it is to explain the nature of valence.

This misreading of Dewey has had a curious effect in American academic life. It has tended to separate those who talk about the processes of teach-ing and learning from those who claim actually to be engaged in teaching and learning. The latter continue to make up the large majority of Ameri-can academics, but the "educationists," most of whom think of themselves as being progressive, have wormed their way into important precincts of the university, where they serve mainly as an inoculation against a serious rethinking of practice. The way it works is this: someone will mention—among historians, or literary scholars, or biologists—the importance of helping students find connections between studies in their discipline and the meaning of ordinary life. And the response, most often will be: "Don't lecture us about that education-school nonsense. Those people don't care anything about real knowledge. They're a gaggle of fuzz-brains who think education is a matter of giving way to childish impulse."

One of the bizarre features of American academics is the faith that if you oppose foolish ideas, your own must be sterling. The scholar of literature who curls his lip at the education department has no answer when he's asked why we need the four-hundredth article of the year on Nathaniel Hawthorne. Because he sees criticism flowing in only one direction, and because he knows that educationism is muddled, he assumes, confidently, that his own modes are beyond reproach.

We can't blame the whole of this false academic dualism on the inelegant prose of a single man. Obviously there are forces at work—mainly the forces of vested interest—which bring on the struggle between proponents of good knowledge and proponents of strong thinking. Yet, Dewey was the most powerful American thinker to try to integrate these essential elements of education. It is worthwhile asking why his thought has not had the influence it should have had, and why his reputation has often been used to thwart the implications of his thought.

In addition to his somniferous style, I can think of two other main reasons, and both of them, indirectly, shed some light on the seeming success of the degree salesmen. The first is that when Dewey turned from educational philosophy to practical political prognostication, things went downhill fast. In the judgment of biographer Robert Westbrook, Dewey's record as a prophet was "dismal." His ideas for reforming society after the First World War were miserably naive. He argued, for example, that centralized authorities could be set up which would not misuse power themselves but would function merely to transfer power from "the more or less rapacious groups now in control." This innocence, which Westbrook says Dewey pre-

ferred to think of as "sinewy optimism," shows forth fulgently in the remarks he made after a trip to the Soviet Union in July of 1928. Although
he was not completely blind to the repressions of the Soviet regime, he did
take the regime at its word. He said of the educational system he observed
in Russia, "In the end, this indoctrination will be subordinate to the awakening of initiative and judgment, while cooperative mentality will be
evolved." When we consider the millions of lives brutalized and wasted by
that government and the limping system bequeathed to the Russian people
of today, we can be glad Dewey never developed overt political ambitions.
The second reason applies to anyone who attempts to address the corruptions of an establishment. He'll be grouped with everybody else who's speaking against the establishment, and, often, with those who scream most fre-
netically. We aren't good in America at making distinctions among critics.
Either you're with the going-system or you're with the people who oppose
it. And there's no doubt that Dewey placed himself in opposition. His educational ideas were driven by his response to the schools he experienced
while growing up. Although they had worthy features, most investigators
today acknowledge that the general schooling practices of the late nineteenth century were rigid, unimaginative, and grounded in a simplistic
morality. Lots of reformers wanted to blast that system apart, and Dewey
was one of them. But they didn't all want to blast it apart for the same end.

Dewey fell victim to a process Robert Westbrook describes accurately in
the introduction of his biography:

> In their eagerness to explore the causes and effects of ideas, Ameri-
> can intellectual historians have often failed to undertake a close
> analysis of the ideas themselves. As a result we have studies that
> explore the origins and impact of ideas that never existed in the
> minds of those thinkers to whom they have been attributed.

The result of this jumbled thinking has been to link Dewey to theorists he,
himself, criticized as "liberal empiricists." He saw them as just as great a
threat to democratic education as conservatives were because they viewed
students as isolated agents of desire, who needed to shape their education

strictly in line with individual impulse. It's clear that if education is to be designed in that way, the needs of society run the risk of being ignored. And this Dewey could not abide. He got around it by pointing out that any desire an individual might have was necessarily linked in some way to his or her social background. Where else could it have come from? It was the teacher's task to make that linkage clear to the student and guide the student towards studies that supported both virtuous social practice and individual meaning. The kind of studies that often take place in progressive settings, where students hop from one topic to another, without much thought given to what any of them mean, he dismissed as frivolous fooling around, which is, indeed, what they are.

All three of these reasons—a flat style of writing, naive political assessments, and guilt by association—have blunted the criticisms Dewey made of schooling practices which, in the colleges and universities at least, have continued to build over the decades since he wrote. This is a shame. I have found no educational thinker who has dealt more precisely and comprehensively with the corruptions being visited on university life by the degree salesmen. You might almost say that Dewey is the objective correlative for the intelligent element of the American left. He has been dumped in a caldron and swirled round with so much unrealistic resentment, weak sentimentalism, and outright cry-babyism that it's very hard either to see or to use him cleanly. If one could, somehow, distill his actual thought from that noxious mixture and bring it to bear on what's occurring in our colleges, we would be a long way towards persuading the degree salesmen to change direction and consider becoming educators. And I think they are, mostly, capable of change because, as I hope I've made clear, they aren't bad people in a conventional sense. They are corrupting the university not out of malice of heart but from misdirection of attention.

If you read extensively in Dewey, you come on so many definitions of education that confound current university practice it's hard to know which ones to mention in a short letter like this. Truth is, you could write books on the subject. I'll pick three that appeal to me, but I do it with the warning that they're no more than a small sample of the Deweyan delineations that indicate what a slight role education plays in the behavior of contemporary institutions.

In *Democracy and Education*, Dewey says that the measure of educative growth is seen in the quality of mental process. Furthermore, if teachers could simply recognize this, it would make for a revolution. So it would. But when the teachers themselves have not been taught, or even urged, to place value on the quality of their own mental processes, it's hard to see how they can convey that concept of education to students. The concentration in most colleges remains on what is taught rather than on what might happen as a result of encountering that material. It's more important to know, for example, that George Washington was president of the United States from 1789 to 1797 than it is to know how to bring that information into relationship with your thoughts so they become richer thereby. I once asked a student this very question: "What does it matter that you know when George Washington was president?" He looked at me like I was from Mars. No one had ever asked him such a thing. He had gone all the way through the American school system, and no one had asked him why it mattered that he knew what he knew. This is a travesty. As Dewey pointed out, repeatedly, it assumes that students are akin to machines. It doesn't perceive them as thinking beings whose thoughts can be made better.

A complementary definition holds education to be a transformation of the quality of experience. Dewey says, in effect, that the educated person will habitually transform the experience in front of him into something more richly complex than it was when he first encountered it. This means that when a student sits down with a teacher to discuss, say, Shakespeare, both of them should have in mind using Shakespeare to make not only their immediate experience finer, but to carry away from their talk about Shakespeare the ability to make subsequent experiences more fulfilling than they would otherwise have been. It also implies that Shakespeare is their topic because he has demonstrated to thousands of readers over hundreds of years an enabling power of enhancing experience. That's why he's read, and talked about, not because we want to be considered cultured, not because learned people have told us that we ought to, but because by doing it we make ourselves more worthy of life. This seems so simple, and so obvious, it would take a cretin not to see it. Yet, go into the classrooms of America and see how often it's observed.

I'll end with a definition that is, perhaps, Dewey's most famous teaching, but also one that has been wildly misunderstood. Dewey argues that education is a thing that results from doing and reflecting upon doing, and not simply from receiving. One feature of his educational writings we need to remember is that, though they are applicable to learning generally, he produced them, primarily, with the teaching and learning of young children in mind. Consequently, when Dewey uses examples (which he doesn't do as much as perhaps he ought), they are usually examples pertinent to the learning of early childhood, when a person is most eager to explore his physical environment. For this reason I suspect a majority of Dewey's readers have applied an unnecessarily restrictive definition to the word "doing." They associate it with tasks like washing the dishes and building a cabinet. They do not associate it with speaking, or reading, or conversing. Yet, these can be forms of doing just as surely as pounding a nail is. And, they are extremely important in education beyond the elementary level because they are the doings we do most.

When two people are having a conversation, it might constitute "doing" from Dewey's point of view, or, it might not. The difference is the quality of concentration on what's being said. If words are simply being received idly and responded to in a lackadaisical way, no "doing" is involved and, therefore, no education is taking place. This is the condition of normal social chatter. If, however, words are being heard attentively, and being reflected upon, and being integrated with other thoughts, before a considered response is made, then education clearly is taking place, and, perhaps, the best education of which we are capable. Because so much of our talk is of the former character, we lose the ability to imagine educative talk, and thereby, we lose the chance of having it. John Dewey wanted the schools to help us recapture that chance.

When Dewey was asked to speak at the dinner honoring his ninetieth birthday, he got up before the fifteen hundred people in attendance and said "Democracy begins in conversation." I'm glad he said that and I wish more people knew that he did. But what I wish most of all is that the administrators and professors in American colleges and universities knew what he meant.

Dewey is the fourth in my list of six educational thinkers. Next comes Lionel Trilling.

*Dalton surprised me by the interest he took in Lionel Trilling.
Though he hadn't paid much attention to Trilling in his heyday,
the critics's stance on the alternative culture fascinated Dalton.
That may speak well for Trilling's ongoing reputation. I hope so
at any rate. He strikes me as a thinker worth continued attention.*

*I*N CHOOSING LIONEL Trilling as my fifth notable thinker, I'm not
implying that he's on a par with the four who have gone before. Trilling has
been dead twenty-six years now and, consequently, finds himself in the
slump that afflicts the reputations of formerly-famous writers in the first
decades after they die. Some of them rise up out of it, and some don't. I'm
not sure what Trilling's fate will be. I must say, though, on re-reading some
of his essays which I hadn't read for years, I think better of him than I had
thought I would.

The book on which I'm basing most of my comments today is a collection
of critical essays titled *Beyond Culture,* which was published in 1965. The
date is significant. It marks the point just before the outbreak of the cultural revolts we think of as having destroyed American innocence, and it
also signals the end of that great intellectual movement known as modernism. It was the last moment when modernism could be dealt with seriously
without taking into account the corrosive beliefs which are now almost
universally designated "postmodernist."

Most of Trilling's writings during the last twenty years of his life took up
the questions of what we mean by the term "culture" and whether it is possible to find a place outside, or "beyond," culture from which we can view it
with a detachment and intelligence that aren't possible inside. It's clear

that for Trilling finding that place is identical with education. In his view those who don't seek it, though they may become technically adept and even learned, are not educated persons.

In his later years, Trilling fell out with many of his former allies because he pointed out that the adversary culture sparked by modernism, the culture to which most of his friends belonged and which set itself in opposition to the general culture of materialism, capitalism, and worship of hierarchy, was nonetheless a culture itself and could be just as cloying and repressive of imagination as the bourgeoisie. Nothing makes a self-proclaimed radical more angry than to be shown up as a conservative within his own little world. I learned that in ways that are branded on my brain through my twelve-year immersion in Goddard College.

In these letters I've taken the stance that the apparent struggle between the professors and the degree salesmen, in the university, mirrors to some extent the battle between the adversary culture and the money worshippers in the general society. Both conflicts are more for show than real. I don't doubt that the participants believe in their own passion, but since it seldom eventuates in action, it's mainly emotion enjoyed for its own sake. Throughout the past, we've seen feigned strife functioning to bolster the status quo, and what's going on in the university nowadays is one more of those instances.

I respect Trilling because he tried to dig beneath the surface pomp and fury to find the forces that actually cause the ground to shift. And he did it always with the problems of teaching and learning in mind. Most of his arguments pertain to the teaching of literature because he was, after all, a professor of literature. Yet, he saw literature as being a more far-reaching activity than his profession has usually been willing to acknowledge. He did his graduate studies in a time when the orthodox position held that literature is art alone and that to think of it in the way of moral instruction is naive. This is an attitude that seems so obviously silly it's hard to believe anyone could ever have taken it seriously. Yet, it was taken seriously, and it affected the way literature was taught and the way professors were produced for quite a number of years. Recently, under assault from feminism and other hyper-moralistic theories, it has subsided, but I don't think its influence is entirely washed away.

An event that forced Trilling to rethink the orthodox stance was the introduction of modern literature into the curriculum at Columbia University. When he began teaching in 1932, no literature produced after the nineteenth century was taught. It was not that the faculty didn't recognize the worth of later writings, but rather that they considered these writings to be of such a different character from what had gone before that they didn't lend themselves to college instruction as it was then understood. The trouble with them was that they were personal, in a deeply psychological way that couldn't be addressed unless a reader brought his own personal issues into contact with them. Trilling displays the attitude of the time when he says that to hold personal considerations out of the teaching of literature is to deal with it in the most "literary" way possible.

As usual, faculty principle gave way to student desire, and modern literature began to be taught at Columbia. What Trilling did about this innovation is the topic of one of his most brilliant essays, "On the Teaching of Modern Literature," which leads off the collection in *Beyond Culture*. It's a complex piece which I can't summarize here. But I can note a couple of its points which complement our conversation. One of Trilling's worries was that modern literature dealt with such deep, black elements of the human psyche that students might not be able to assimilate it. But he found that they assimilated it very well. As he says:

> I asked them to look into the Abyss, and both dutifully and gladly, they have looked into the Abyss, and the Abyss has greeted them with the grave courtesy of all objects of serious study, saying: "Interesting, am I not?"

Trilling seems to have forgotten—or to have missed—the very effective training which teaches students to keep classroom subjects inside the classroom, to denature them so to speak, so that though they might have their little fascinations, they're not going to sneak out and hit you when you go home. It would be neurotic to think of this as the effect of conspiracy, yet it operates in a conspiratorial way to protect both faculty members and degree salesmen from having to think deeply about the nature of education. If education were seen not just as classroom exercise but as a force that radiated out to all aspects of life, students would begin to demand that it add substance, and excitement, and satisfaction to their everyday experience. The university, in turn, would have to respond to the demand by reorganizing the curriculum and by rethinking how to interact with it.

Having noted that students can dutifully take in almost anything, Trilling goes on to comment that we can't, after all, expect them in their written exercises to say anything vital. As he puts it, "a term-essay is not an occasion for telling the truth." What is it an occasion for, then? He suggests that the most we can expect is a "proper response" to the teaching of the professor. Without worrying ourselves too much about the difference between a proper response and an improper one (this is the sort of distinction Trilling, being a professor, appears to believe is self-evident), we still ought to be able to ask: a proper response to what end? Why is it that students are consuming untold reams of paper to produce writings that virtually all professors hate to read? Are they simply exercises designed to improve technical skills? Are they instruments for demonstrating dutiful reading, and, if they are, to whom is the duty being paid? Are they things people do because they can't think of anything else to do in the process of awarding degrees? None of these is a good enough reason for the effort consumed in the process.

I have to believe that Trilling said some of this tongue-in-cheek. He was too good a teacher not to know that the prime justification for student writing is to lead people towards careful conversation that will aid them in coming to know their own hearts and minds. He was also, however, one of those critics who make such deep bows towards the enemy (to show he understands their position) that he, sometimes, almost falls over into their camp. The enemy in this case was an over-ripe modernism veering toward the position that the very concept of a worthy self is an outmoded romanticism, that there is no self to be known or realized, that people are simply accidents created by environmental collisions. Everybody must have toyed with that idea from time to time. But when you toy with it, you also have to recognize that it nullifies any prospect of education and turns the idea of it into an absurdity.

Knowing one's own mind, or coming to construct a self, as we say nowadays, is a controversial concept that philosophers wrangle over endlessly. I'll try, briefly, to relate it to my arguments in the next letter. Here I'll say only that without a self to be built there is no education to be had, or, at least, no education that comports with traditional values. Trilling's goal was to examine those traditional values in an effort to discover how the modern adversary culture had mistaken them, or lost the language to talk about them gracefully. He wanted to restore them, but to restore them in a way that left them free of the stuffy, hypocritical moralizing they had formerly been thought to entail.

A part of his tactic was to re-read authors we are, more or less, bound to respect, but who have been virtually dismissed from the modern debate by the notion that though they were good for their time, their time has passed, and so they can no longer serve as vital voices in helping us know what to do in our own time. They can be read now, but they are read for escape, and as examples of artistry. This, by the way, is one of the more foolish arguments the academy has entertained, and it has done as much as anything to emasculate the curriculum and turn it into the corporate training program the degree salesmen seek increasingly to peddle.

I think my favorite example of this tactic is the essay "*Emma* and the Legend of Jane Austen," which serves for me as a model of the way critical writing can be lifted out of academic fustiness and brought into social and political discourse. *Emma*, says Trilling, is generally regarded as Jane Austen's finest novel. I guess he's right about that. I often recall Ronald Blythe's remark, in the introduction of one of the older Penguin editions, that *Emma* is the Parthenon of fiction. But why is it the Parthenon of fiction? Trilling answers that it is a very subtle and difficult novel, so difficult that most critics have been unable to face up to it. Jane Austen's legend, as a delightful writer of tales about the romantic adventures of young women in a time quaint and never to be recovered, has obscured the vital message about the nature of morality that lies at the heart of the novel. Certainly the most famous thing ever said about *Emma* was said by the author, who remarked that she had created a character whom no one but herself was apt to like. And this has been taken as one of her fabled ironies because, in fact, most readers have liked Emma. The trouble is, they haven't known why. She's a snob; she's a meddler; she fouls up other people's lives; she does no socially productive work, at least as work is regarded today. So what is it we like about her?

Trilling says we like her because she supplies a need we don't even know we have. We don't know we have it because we believe, or we have been taught, that we can take refuge from ourselves in the citadel of commonplace life. And this is a lie. Commonplace life is no refuge against the demons of self. In truth, it's the hell those demons have built for us. What we need to escape it is some great good place in our own imagination to which we can resort. He quotes Schiller from his essay "On Simple and Sentimental Poetry" to the effect that an idyllic retreat is essential for a sane life. It is a vision that tells us where we are going, or where we ought to be going. And *Emma* offers us that idyll because it presents a world set away from genuine sordidness, where life can be lived both vividly and sanely, if one has the intelligence to educate herself, which Emma, despite all her faults, clearly does have.

My purpose here is not to assert Trilling's critical accuracy, or even to stand behind the philosophy of Schiller and Jane Austen (although on other occasions I would be happy to stand up for them). I want, instead, to point to how Trilling leads us, through literature, to practices that are vital to good living. If we do not read good books and then have searching conversations about them, how are we to know what's vital for good living? Are we presumed to have been born with that knowledge in our heads? That would seem to be the position of people who dismiss genuine education as frivolity. They are dreadfully wrong.

One of Trilling's favorite quotations, which he cites repeatedly, comes from a letter John Keats wrote to his brother and sister in the spring of 1819. He was musing on the possibility that a thought might be fine, though it is imperfect and even marked by error. And then he wrote, "This is the very thing in which consists poetry; and if so it is not so fine a thing as philosophy—For the same reason as an eagle is not so fine a thing as a truth."

Trilling uses this to suggest that the great books, fine as they are, may not always lead us to the right place. We can use them amiss. For that reason we always have to be thinking about how to use them better. Thinking of that kind, which always takes place by sharing our thoughts, is what I'm trying to defend here as the essence of education. Trilling has helped me do it more than most people I've read.

I haven't done as much with the making of the self as perhaps I should. I'll try to remedy that next time by taking a look at Charles Taylor. He's not as famous as my other five thinkers, but among contemporary writers he has more intelligent things to say about the problems of education than anyone else I've found. He'll be the final figure in my abbreviated survey of thinkers, and then we'll have to go on to something else.

With Charles Taylor, I introduced ideas that are more philosophically exotic than those of the other educational thinkers I discussed. I was hesitant to do it because I didn't want to alienate intelligent general readers. Yet Taylor makes such important points about the nature of the selves we're trying to get by with in the world today that I couldn't leave him out. Besides, with a little extra attention, his ideas become very clear.

I CHOSE CHARLES Taylor as the final figure on this brief tour of thinkers because, as much as anything I've read, his books helped me sort out questions that have puzzled me since I began teaching. In the last letter I said that unless people have some notion of forging selves out of the package of genetic material handed them at birth, education can have little genuine meaning for them. If they assume that learning is simply a matter of acquiring skills and tools that will be used by the same old selves, all the way through, then most serious thinking devoted to education loses significance. If, however, they view education as self-formation, then defining its character becomes an integral element of life.

The problem with self-formation, as with education, is that you can't know in advance exactly what you're seeking. If you could, you would already be most of the way there, and education would be no more than acquiring disciplines to help the self prevail. There wouldn't be much discovery about it. Yet, in the definition of education I've been arguing for, discovery is the main thing. So, the question becomes: what can be discovered pertaining to self-formation that will assist a person towards a self that's satisfying and fulfilling? That's where Charles Taylor comes in.

Taylor is a Canadian philosopher who taught for a portion of his career at Oxford. In 1989, he published a very big and, I think, important book titled *Sources of the Self: The Making of the Modern Identity.* It's significant for a number of reasons, but for our purposes its importance lies mainly in the way it connects the self to concepts of right and wrong. Taylor could not be more clear or firm about this linkage. As he says:

> To know who you are is to be oriented in moral space, a space in which questions arise about what is good or bad, what is worth doing and what not, what has meaning and importance for you and what is trivial and secondary.

The way you answer these questions determines who you are, far more than any natural or sociological category you may inhabit. There's a notion abroad in America that questions of this kind can be answered instinctively and, therefore, they don't have to be thought about. We don't have to ask, for example, what is good; we simply have to ask how to get it. Taylor confronts this idea head on, and as far as I'm concerned, destroys it so thoroughly that no sensible person who read his account would attempt to resurrect it. Anybody who wants to know how he carries out the demolition needs to read his book, which isn't an easy task. In this letter, I'm simply going to take it as established that you aren't born with any personal knowledge of a good life, and that if you don't work to educate yourself about it, you never will know what it is.

What you do get, of course, through the process of growing up, is a set of assumptions about right and wrong which is handed to you by your society. The term Taylor uses for assumptions about the most important things of life is moral "framework," and the early portion of his analysis consists of describing what frameworks are and how they come into being. There have been societies of the past—ancient Egypt, for example—in which, as far as we know, almost everyone accepted the same framework. Consequently, there was little occasion for fundamental dispute. That clearly is no longer the case. Taylor tells us that no framework forms the horizon for the whole society of the modern West. In truth, there are so many frameworks we can't count them all. Everyone is confronted, sooner or later, with deciding what framework he or she will inhabit and whether this is merely a matter of picking one from the many available or of building one for the self.

The great danger, in this condition of modern individualism, is that one will, willy nilly, fall into a framework that doesn't adequately accommodate his own character or that divides him from society in a destructive way. He will then, as we say, be alienated.

When personal and social frameworks fail to overlap significantly, a person is presented with a problem. As the area of overlap becomes smaller, the problem becomes more acute. Trying to maintain oneself in that area, a person feels increasingly squeezed, and, for some, the pressure becomes intolerable. Then we have the outbreaks that we wring our hands about and call inexplicable. In actuality, they aren't inexplicable at all; they are inherent in the systems we keep trying to force down our own throats.

The dramatic manifestations of this process, such as Timothy McVeigh, are merely the surface of a deep social effect. People ask why there's so much anger in our world? This is the reason.

What can we do about it? Taylor's answer is that we can understand the identities we inhabit. We can understand where they came from; we can understand the implications they force upon us; we can understand whom they serve and whom they hurt. This, in a way, is simply a detailed explication of the Socratic dictum to know ourselves. I certainly agree with that answer, and I think education is a method for realizing it. Since Taylor is not writing specifically about education, he says relatively little about what we can do with what we know. Maybe he thinks that's evident. My experience has been, though, that it is not evident, that knowing is one part of education and knowing what to do is another. When we know we are squeezed, and when we know why we are squeezed, it simply induces anger unless we can think of ways to shift the frameworks so that the overlap expands and gives us more room to live.

Taylor assists us here by pointing out that a self can exist only among other selves. He says we construct selves in "webs of interlocution" (a point I haven't made about him till now is that though he's a serviceable writer, better I think than Dewey, he is not always eloquent). This means we make ourselves who we are by interacting with other people and, mainly, by asking and answering questions. It's the same point I've been trying to make throughout these letters, that education takes place in an environment where critical conversation can occur. The degree salesmen, to the extent they think of anything other than selling paper credentials, concentrate on hiding from this truth because offering a good environment for critical conversation doesn't fit with their ideas of cost containment. It is cheaper to provide pre-packaged clumps of information, and easier to market them as well.

If we accept Taylor's point that we build ourselves by exchanging questions and answers with others, it follows that the quality of the questions and answers becomes crucial. A moral framework is defined partly by the questions that circulate within it. By seeking out different questions, we move ourselves into different frameworks, and we create the possibility that a new framework can give us more room to live than the old one did. If we move, for example, from asking how to kick ass through accounting to how to assess the cost of a particular idealism, we encounter a different set of moral responsibilities and we gain a different set of companions. Our personal framework moves into a different territory, and not only that; it finds itself overlapping with a different social perspective.

Knowing this doesn't tell us the direction we should move. That depends on what Taylor calls our "hypergoods," that is the goods that rise above all others, the goods we cannot deny or desert no matter what tests we subject them to. Probably the most important philosophical point made by *Sources of the Self* is that we all have a number of hypergoods and that they don't always agree with one another. The good of loving someone devoutly, for example, which was the prime good of the society I grew up in, does not comport with the good of full self-development, which has become the prime good of the society I now inhabit. That conflict has become so acute, it has pervaded popular culture, although popular culture doesn't know that's what it is. It forms the moral background of the TV series *Ally McBeal, Judging Amy, Family Law,* and to a lesser extent of *West Wing.*

Much of Taylor's argument is spent on showing how various intellectual schemes have attempted to dissolve the conflict between hypergoods and bring them into unity. The one that draws the most intense scrutiny is what Taylor calls modernity's "procedural ethic," that is the idea that though we can never agree on what's really good we can adopt a series of behavioral rules which determine how we shall interact with our fellow creatures. The trouble with this is that it often produces consequences we know are not right, and the only way we can abide them is pretend that right in a universal sense doesn't exist, and that our best approximation of it is right rule. This pretense is the target of Taylor's most scathing commentary. For example:

> This is what has been suppressed by these strange cramped theories of modern moral philosophy, which have the paradoxical effect of making us inarticulate on some of the most important issues of morality. Impelled by the strongest metaphysical, epistemological, and moral ideas of the modern age, these theories narrow our focus to the determinants of action, and then restrict our understanding of these determinants still further by defining practical reason as exclusively procedural. They utterly mystify the priority of the moral by identifying it not with substance but with a form of reasoning, around which they draw a firm boundary. They then are led to defend this boundary all the more fiercely in that it is their only way of doing justice to the hypergoods which move them although they cannot acknowledge them.

He's right about that. I find myself increasingly frustrated by a willingness to countenance the most deplorable outcomes so long as they were produced by established procedures. The courts often seem to say that it's all right for the state to kill an innocent man so long as no procedures were violated in convicting him. This is, at bottom, arguing that humans are no more than machines, and that if we try to treat them as being other than

machines we'll foul up our systems. It is the source of the nauseating pae-
ans to "the rule of law" we have heard so much of lately. It is a complete
denial of the possibility of education.

The question for Taylor (and for me) is what is superior to rule-based life?
His answer employs another of his peculiar locutions, a concept he calls
"the exploration of order through personal resonance." What is "personal
resonance" as Taylor uses it? It is a perceiving in something outside ourselves a worth that's greater than our own personal fulfillment. It strikes
me as being a kind of gnosis, that is, a knowledge that can't be denied,
which tells us that something is incomparably worthy, that it cannot be
deserted. Taylor doesn't use the word "gnosis," I suspect, because he wants
to avoid its association with a kind of mysticism he deplores. And yet, the
thing he's talking about involves perceptions that are difficult to explain.
We have these perceptions most often nowadays about the natural environment. We cannot let lions vanish from the face of the earth, for example,
even though they're not doing us any good from an instrumental point of
view. But, we cannot abandon them, and if we do, we'll know that we have
failed ourselves in a most disgraceful way. We will have been unfaithful to a
grandeur that deserves our loyalty. Taylor is telling us, in effect, that we
should base our actions on that kind of loyalty more than on anything else.

I agree, and yet I know that there is great danger in gnosis, or in "personal
resonance" (Taylor by the way, knows this too). It lies in the truth that all
sorts of prejudices and bigotries can try to pass themselves off as special or
revealed knowledge. If we accept their self-proclamation we open ourselves
to any manner of horror. This is where education has to step in. Education,
being a process of vigorous questioning, gives us a chance, in effect, to vet
any assertion of special moral knowledge and any claim to an unassailable
integrity of selfhood. We can subject them to the most searching examination, we can set them up against any hypergood anyone can bring to mind,
we can test them by time and history. Only after they have passed the most
rigorous challenges we can put in their paths do they have the right to social standing. But once a proposition has met these tests we can be pretty
sure we have something of value. The process of winnowing though de-

mands critical education. It doesn't happen quickly or without patience. Obviously, the university isn't the only place for it. It can happen anywhere intelligent and fair-minded people engage one another. But the university does bear a special responsibility towards it because the university continues in the mind of the general public to be the arena where people are supposed to learn how to separate good arguments from foolishness.

I've now completed the survey of thinkers I promised. Each of the six—Newman, Emerson, Arnold, Dewey, Trilling, and Taylor—is so much more subtle and complex than I've been able to suggest that I worry I've been unfaithful to them. But then I reflect that I didn't set out to explain who they were or to explicate their thought. All I wanted was to find out whether their general definitions of education had anything in common with the thoughts I've been trying to develop here. And, low and behold, they do, not because I've been original, but because all of them have been my teachers in ways I can never fully recognize.

The point I want to end with today is that when we look at a half-dozen notable thinkers who have garnered the respect of millions of readers over two centuries and discover that none of them has anything to say supportive of the kind of schooling that is being pushed by the majority of current college and university managers, it gives us the right, at least, to be suspicious of what the latter are doing. I sense that my own suspicions, if not established, are not utterly berserk, and I'm encouraged to continue working with them.

To return to the matter of frameworks. They are defined, in part, by the discourse they offer us. I'd rather be in a framework with the six men I've talked about over the last few weeks than with most of the persons I've known in so-called real life, even when the latter are the occupants of exalted academic positions. Still, I like to have discourse with anybody. But you have to get it where you can find it.

Another letter will be along shortly.

At this point I began the last full section of the series, six letters designed to show that education becomes pertinent to the lives people are required to live by demanding attention to aspects of life many think they can ignore.

*A*S I APPROACH the final stretch of this effort, I run against the truth that a limitless subject forces hard choices at the end. What I've wanted to do with the whole series is show that education as it's been defined by the best minds who have dealt with it is getting scanty attention from the managers of colleges and universities in America. They're turning the university away from education towards something else, which they think is easier to market: a combination of credentialism and weak career preparation. Their motivation isn't an educational ideal but a concept of managerial success in which income production is the first goal. I've called them degree salesmen because that's what they are.

I've tried to make this point in several ways, and now I've reached the stage where I can make it in only one other way if I'm going to stay within the limits I set for myself. A part of me asks: "Hell, why not just go on writing to Dalton forever?" There are at least a million things the degree salesmen are doing to transmogrify the university. I could try to expose them all and write a letter a week till I die. I can imagine worse things to do. But that would be to impose on your patience and wear out your spectacles, neither of which would be seemly. So, I've got to finish with this letter plus seven more, which requires that I decide what to treat in the little space I have left.

Having thought about it, the best I can do is rely on the definition I've pursued till now, that is, education as a mode of being that strengthens all areas of life. If my definition is apt, I should be able to look at life's common areas and show both how education would make them healthier and how current university behavior subverts what the university ought to be doing with respect to them. I'll start with politics and government.

In an age of political cynicism, like the one we're in now, quite a few people try to wash their hands of politics. It's all crap and crookedness, they say. They don't want anything to do with it. People who talk that way need to be reminded that they're going to have something to do with it, whether they want to or not. Every human being lives in a political environment which affects his life for good and ill. You can say, of course, that you'll simply accept the consequences whatever they are and pay no attention to the institutions that produced them. But, it's probably not possible actually to do it, and it's clearly not possible for anyone who deserves to be considered an educated person. Participation in political affairs is a necessity for the educated mind.

This is so obvious it seems impossible to understand why anybody thinks he can ignore politics. In fact, it is hard to understand unless we pay attention to the historical evolution of ideas. One of the most depressing features of political culture is that institutions and attitudes live on long after the theories that gave them birth have been either discredited or forgotten. In America, this problem is particularly acute because modern America, perhaps foremost among all societies, has disabled its memory, with the degree salesmen taking the lead. Few now recall that just two generations ago our ideas were dominated by Marxist social analysis. When I say "dominated" I don't mean everybody agreed with it but, rather, that it supplied the body of thought about which people argued. The big issue was whether Marxism was right or wrong, good or wicked. When ideas are widely debated, they seep into the minds even of those who oppose them and remain there as a residue. The principal deposits that Marxism left in the Western mind are the beliefs that liberal politics exist simply as a ruse to cover the activities of hidden economic forces and that the political state as we know it must wither away if perfect justice is to be had. These ideas gained their potency because, despite their deeply flawed nature, there's an element of truth in both of them. And that element has worked, not only to create an anti-democratic caretaker state but, more disastrously, to foster the belief that it is wiser than we are and that it can be serviced by professionals independent of serious public discussion of its essential nature. Whenever you hear people say, resignedly, "Well, that's just the way things are now," you can be sure both that these ideas are having an influence and that the speaker has no inkling where they came from.

I know I risk being thought a historical fanatic. But, I can't help it. All my experience teaches me that social ill comes from the puppet-like behavior of people who don't know the source of their ideas. As they run away from the truth of the past, they run towards ill-considered and shallow responses to current difficulties. Somebody blows up a public building? Let's put a guard at every public doorway. Then we can feel more secure. This is about the level of thought driving politics today. We indulge ourselves in it because we don't want to examine the truths of political behavior. The degree salesmen in their program for building the university discourage attention to a search for the origins of our attitudes and beliefs. Without that search standing at the core of the university's mission, higher education will do little to promote a more just or a freer society.

Another major truth we need to face, which is denied by almost every major politician in America, is that a person's political stance is affected dramatically by his personal situation. There's no political position derivable from disinterested reason. Every now and then someone will ask me why I'm not a Republican, and I invariably reply that I don't have enough money to be a Republican. It's only partly a joke. The major political division in every society lies between those who have wealth and privilege and those who don't. The wealthy want to hold on to what they have and increase it. The poor want to get something for themselves. There's virtually no self-deception people won't take up, and no hypocrisy they won't adopt, in pursuit of these desires. In the midst of their hypocrisy they forget that the primary mission of politics is to prevent each side from inflicting irreparable damage on the other.

An accepted political lie in America is that we're all striving together to make the best country possible. But that's sweet talk with no meaning. The best country for whom? The best country for the CEO of a financial institution who spends most of his time figuring out how to make deals, for example, won't be the best country for me. He wants a different life than I want, and, therefore, he wants laws that will sponsor his life, not mine. Conflict of that kind is inevitable, so long as we don't all become robotic copies of one another.

Educated thought directs us to face reality. When we acknowledge it, we have a chance of discovering how to diminish its current toxicity. Since there really are both rich and poor people, and since their financial interests are, to some extent, opposed, we can, if we confront the truth, seek a system where the one will hurt the other as little as possible. It's easier, and more civil actually, to deal with an opponent who acknowledges his own interests than it is with one who smarms you with the falsehood that he has your interests at heart. In politics, people are sympathetic to your interests as long as you help them become richer and more powerful. As soon as you do anything to jeopardize their position, even if it's for your own vital interests, their sympathy disappears. Recognizing the bitter hardness of political strife is the only thing likely to maintain an interest in mollifying it.

Karl von Clausewitz's famous dictum, that war is simply the continuation of politics by other means, would be just as true if it were turned around. In fact, there's some value in reversing it because when we think about moving from war to politics we see that it happens only when enemies reach the conclusion that the cost of the contest is greater than any benefit victory might confer. People generally go to war because they don't accurately calculate the cost. Might we say that they go to politics for the same reason?

A source of social distress in America today is our having politicized issues that aren't amenable to political solutions. Our famed war on drugs is just the most blatant example. When we do this we create two classes of evil: we make non-political problems worse, and we take intelligent attention away from the issues that require political treatment. Educated minds have the duty of making fine and accurate distinctions. Right now, political life is marked by their absence and, certainly, by a general inattention to the fundamental purposes of government or the costs associated with them. We do, of course, gripe about taxes and try to shift them onto somebody else, but that's just trying to make deals for ourselves and our buddies. It's not political thought.

The departmentalized structure of the university, which exists for marketing purposes and for providing security for a professionalized faculty, thwarts the possibility of a comprehensive examination of the political situation. I'm not saying that an occasional good teacher doesn't attempt something of that kind in the privacy of his or her classroom, but it is not any longer a common activity in the university, and most graduates leave without having devoted any serious thought to the nature of the political state.

Most Americans used to know Patrick Henry's pre-eminent warning, but the hordes of students now devoting themselves to morally flaccid management techniques and ever more curious forms of self-indulgence are not likely to be taught much about vigilance of any sort. It is not an attribute the corporate world admires, and as the university becomes more and more its adjunct, there will be fewer occasions for mentioning it on our campuses. Yet anyone who has paid even a cursory attention to the history of state power should recognize the validity of Henry's aphorism. Why is it that most American youth think that they are immune to history's common infections and can happily spend their lives in a quest for new cars and stock options? I suspect it's because almost no one has thought to teach them that they are a part of history. In America, history is something that happens to other people. If the university has any duty at all, it is clearly to rout fulsome innocence of that kind. Yet, no attack is taking place.

In Tolstoy's *War and Peace*, Prince Andrei Bolkonsky says prophetically, "If everyone would only fight for his own convictions there would be no wars." There then follow about fourteen hundred pages showing how agonizingly right he was. We can apply the same insight to politics and say that if we had the government most people believe in there would be relatively little injustice. We don't have such a government because, over the past couple generations, it has grown not through discourse among the citizens about what they really believe but through special deals, catering to vested interests, and the inattention of people who think they're too busy to investigate the nature of the structures growing around them.

Consider, as an example, the federal tax code. It is generally thought to be so flawed as to be disgusting. The citizens of the United States live in fear of it, as attested by the flood of nervous jokes that begin to pepper television programming in March of every year. To administer it, Congress has created an agency with a potential for tyranny unrivalled in our history. That it is not as tyrannical as it might be we owe not to current political thought or behavior, and certainly not to any cultural decency, but to the constitutional restraints put in place more than two hundred years ago by men who did engage in serious political debate.

If the American people think they can continue to rely on those restraints, without bothering to understand the document that contains them or the political theories that brought it into being, they are wallowing in one of history's greatest eruptions of foolishness.

We might think that when foolishness is afoot in the land we could rely on the universities to come into the field as our champions. But take a survey among our degree salesmen and see how many are recommending studies in political thought and the nature of constitutional government. I pay fairly close attention to the promotional materials flowing from the universities and I have seen almost nothing of that kind. Announcements of substantial political studies are dwarfed by the flood of materials promising easy learning through electronic techniques to enable students to move into easy money.

In *Habits of the Heart*, a book about American thought patterns, published fifteen years ago by a group of sociological and religious scholars, the general conclusion was that the American people lack the language to speak clearly to one another about their deepest concerns. This is doubtless true of most areas of life, but of none is it more true than of politics. Our political efforts are inefficient because we don't know how to frame intelligent political discussion. Anyone who doesn't think this is true should switch on the late night talk shows. Education is the means for creating discussions that can make genuine differences, and it was once thought that a primary responsibility of university education was to supply the citizens with language and concepts by which they could fashion a government in accordance with their moral beliefs. There is no doubt that the university has turned away from that responsibility, or that the reason for turning away is a bloated desire to sell credentials.

Next time, I'll go on to another common feature of life. I'm planning to deal with five more, before turning to some general thoughts about the series in my last two letters.

The dangers of a sentimental nationalism have become ever more acute since I wrote this letter. There's probably no area in which education is more needed, and right now more lacking, than in teaching Americans how to love their country intelligently.

*I*T'S CURIOUS THAT most Americans appear to be severely cynical about politics while remaining very romantic about the American nation. It's as though, in their minds, the government is not really a valid representation of national reality. The government can be sordid, cheap, and mindless without diminishing national grandeur.

There's a way in which that's true but also a way in which it's not. Being clear about the difference is a chief duty of citizenship, one I don't think the universities are helping people discharge either honorably or effectively.

A person's identity as a member of a nation is currently the most powerful element of self-recognition. One is an American even before one is black or white, man or woman, believer or atheist. We don't consciously know that's how we see ourselves, but it's how most people's perception works. Since it is, our sense of what it means to be an American is a potent factor in determining behavior and, therefore, ought to attract considerable educational scrutiny. Yet, the university curriculum gives it almost no attention.

A couple generations ago, the subject was at least touched on in historical study, which most educated people considered essential for a mature sensibility. But lately, historical investigation has faded in curricular importance to the point the average graduate has less than a trivial understanding of the nation's past or, for that matter, of the past of humankind. I saw a report just last week that fewer than half the current college graduates can identify the language spoken by Caesar and Cicero. And even in my own teaching environs I heard a lively argument a while back about whether it was reasonable to expect elementary school teachers to know which country the United States used atomic bombs against during the Second World War. The person who said it shouldn't be expected was a trainer of teachers.

Throughout history, being human has involved membership in a group and finding personal meaning in service to the group. In recent times there has been idealistic talk about group loyalty being replaced by devotion to universal "human" rights. But it's not a realistic prospect. Humans aren't constructed to care about all people equally. And once we pass beyond personal affection the thing that holds us most strongly is common nationality.

So, here's this powerful feeling that tells us who we are, and whom we should care about, and how we should behave, and yet we don't seriously examine it in our schools, or in our political debates, or in the media. It's as though everybody knows what to do about it without ever being taught.

The expectation of unexamined loyalty is an invitation for abuse. Even Dr. Johnson, who was generally a great booster of all things British, remarked on the eve of the American Revolution that "Patriotism is the last refuge of the scoundrel." In America, over the two and a quarter centuries since that time, the amount of pure nastiness that's been excused by the cry of national security has made a chronicle that can never be told because it's too damned long.

I am not, as you know, a left-wing person. My unwillingness to celebrate leftist sensibilities has cost me a good deal of favor in the places I've worked. I haven't discovered along the liberal-radical portion of the political spectrum greater decency or intelligence than I've found anywhere else. I'm aware that the exercise of national power requires, upon occasion, hard actions and, sometimes, even the spending of lives. I recognize that under the pressure of the moment honorable people who are trying to do the right thing are driven to behavior that doesn't stand up well to subsequent examination, and so I'm willing to give them the benefit of the doubt in judging what they did. Even so, I can't escape the truth that over the past several decades the United States government, under the cover of a blind nationalism, has done things that no reasonable person could approve and that could not have been done had the people of the United States been educated to the level we have the right to expect from the wealth we have poured into our schools and universities. Is this the fault of the institutions and the degree salesmen? Well, if it's not their fault, whose is it?

I'll give just one example of what I mean. In December of 1989, the United States launched an assault against the people of Panama, killed an uncounted number of them (probably at least three thousand), destroyed the homes of twenty thousand people, put thousands into concentration camps, imprisoned some for as long as a year and half without ever bringing any charges against them, and shoveled hundreds of unidentified bodies into large graves and covered them over with bulldozers. What was the reason given for these actions? The political leader of Panama, a former lackey of the United States who over the course of twenty years had been paid hundreds of thousands of dollars by the taxpayers of the United States, had become uncooperative. It was said he was dealing in drugs, which, with the full knowledge of U.S. authorities, he had been doing all the time he was receiving American payments. The very planes the United States paid for to carry weapons, through Panama, to Central America were also used to carry drugs out of Central America to the United States. But, supposedly, this man, who wasn't behaving much differently than he had ever behaved, had become such a threat to American security that the United States arrogated to itself the right to kill thousands of Panamanian citizens—civilians, not soldiers—destroy millions of dollars worth of Panamanian property, and violate international law in a way that subsequently brought condemnation from the United Nations. The code name under which these actions were carried out was "Operation Just Cause."

Anyone who is uncertain about the character of what happened in Panama should look at a documentary film titled *Panama Deception*, which won the Academy Award in 1993 and was directed by Barbara Trent of "The Empowerment Project," a foundation in Chapel Hill, North Carolina, which reports on the behavior of the U.S. media. In it, dozens of people are interviewed, and not just those you would expect to have a knee-jerk hostility to the United States. A former admiral of the U.S. Navy and a retired official of the C.I.A. explain in chilling detail what was done and what the motives for it were.

I don't think those motives would be acceptable if they were ever explained to the people of the United States. But, for the most part, the people have not heard them because they swallowed whole the story given them by the Bush administration. Not only did the general citizenry fail to inquire about what really went on in Panama, our fabled press, which is supposedly the bulwark of our liberty, did an abominable job of reporting the situation. Very little attention was given to the killing of civilians or to the systematic burning of private homes. Day after day, Pete Williams, the White House press secretary, got up and denied U.S. actions, and he was never seriously called to account.

My point here is educational, not political. An educated people does not allow its government to do things of this kind without asking serious questions about them. Nor do they forget what was done as rapidly as we do. We can be pretty sure that the eight year old boy who saw his mother incinerated by the U.S. Army, and who is now coming to manhood, has not forgotten it. The press blithely uses the terms "terrorist" and "terrorist threat" as though these phenomena were akin to typhoid fever. You'll wait a long time before you hear Dan Rather explain to you that a terrorist is someone who hates us, and is prepared to sacrifice his life to hurt us, because of the things our government has done to people he cares about. An educated populace would reflect that we, at least in part, create the terrorists, and that we would be well advised to create as few as possible. If they become too numerous, no defensive measures we take can be effective against them. The best national security comes from behaving in such a way that relatively few people want to destroy you.

I realize that every government, from time to time, does disgusting things. That seems to be the nature of governments. When great power is concentrated in a few hands, as it always is where governments are concerned, manias and insane ideologies can take over and drive policy. There is no reason to think that our government is exempt from the general condition. But, we have told ourselves that because we have a vigilant press and an informed citizenry the United States government is less likely to descend to filthy behavior than other governments of history. That's probably true, as long as the press and the citizens are vigilant and informed. But when they are bottled up by money on the one hand and ignorance on the other, our safeguards are eviscerated.

It is one thing, of course, to see that your own government is a part of the history of governments, and therefore in need of restraint, and another to get caught up in a kind of inverse romanticism which holds your own government to be the worst there ever was. The latter has been the general practice of much left-wing rhetoric in America, and it has been just as strong an enemy of reasoned investigation as blowhard patriotism has— and perhaps even more so. The reason is that no decent person wants to be allied with voices that hate his own people. When a wave of propaganda can find nothing good in either the American government or the American people, it will be rejected out of hand, and the elements of truth that are contained in its criticism will be contemned just as heartily as the lies. That has generally been the effect of the Left in American politics. It disarms valid criticism by mixing it up with so much scum few can stand the odor of the compound.

What the Left finds easy to forget is that there is a form of nationalism which every intelligent person has not only the right but the duty to espouse. We derive not only our sense of ethics but our vision of the good life from the experiences we have of growing up in a certain time and place. If we can't find something to love in that time and place, we will never do good of any sort. We will never have a soul; it's not the sort of thing you can go into the mall of nations and buy for yourself.

The attitude that most divides me from some of my patronizing acquaintances is that they can find nothing to celebrate in American popular life. They don't like hot dogs, and they haven't been to a ball game, ever. They don't care who wins the World Series or the Super Bowl. They don't even care whether Shaquille O'Neil or Kobe Bryant is the man. They've never seen a Clint Eastwood movie, and they won't look at old John Wayne re-runs because he was in favor of U.S. policy in Vietnam. They don't know the difference between *Law and Order* and *NYPD Blue;* they don't even know who Diane was on *Cheers*. They've never been to Nashville or to Jackson, Mississippi, and they can't imagine going to Little Rock. They don't own a single tape of Loretta Lynn, or Dolly Parton; they've never listened to Emmy Lou Harris. They didn't like Elvis when he was alive, and they still don't think he contributed much to American musicology. They would be horrified by the thought of eating at McDonald's. They've never swum across a river, had a fist fight, or chucked an orange at anybody's head. They've never owned a Ford or Chevrolet. They've never been in the Army or shined their shoes so they would pass inspection. They don't know how the ex-Cub factor works. They won't drink Coke. I could go on, but you get the point.

Perhaps the prime characteristic of the miseducated mind is that it makes false associations. It assumes that things have to go together which have no reasoned affinity for one another. It connects love of country with a puffed-up patriotism which can see no fault in American foreign policy. It links minor cultural tastes with major ethical stands. It puts intelligence in the same box as geographical origin. It equates ignorance about common things with a deep appreciation of rare things. It will not permit intelligent distinction or seeing things only for what they are and no more.

Nationalism is a friend of miseducation when it becomes a defender, or rationalizer, of all the things a nation is, or does. And an automatic hostility to the nation is an ironic ally of it. A nation, being a creature of history, should not be viewed as an instrument either of God or the Devil. We need to know clearly where it came from, what it has done, what potential for both good and evil resides in its composition. This is the kind of knowledge higher education ought to help us attain. Only when we have examined the actuality of our national heritage can we have a chance of directing the future away from its unfortunate characteristics and towards those that do it honor. If I could make only one point on this topic it would be that a nation can be well-served only by people who love it but don't worship it. There's a reason, after all, why the first commandment comes first.

I said at the beginning that we need to be able to tell the difference between our nation as a cultural force and as a political entity. That's because we need to be able to love and shape the one, and examine and constrain the other. To make that distinction, and to see clearly what each of these things is, requires careful curricular planning and the best habits of the critical mind. Right now, I can't see that the universities are devoted sincerely to either.

I think I've said enough now about the political aspect of education. I'm planning to devote the rest of the letters on educational application to what might be called the intimate factors of life.

Jean Paul Sartre is famed for having said that hell is other people. We've tended more to agree with him than to ask why that's indeed the case. The attitude discussed in this letter is a good part of the reason.

*H*AVING BEGUN WITH government and nationalism, in laying out some applications of education, I'll now shift focus and turn to intimate topics. I don't mean to say the subjects I have in mind are intimate in the sense of lacking a public face. In reality, their public manifestations make up the greater part of our social atmosphere. But, they're intimate because they go to the core of how we feel about and judge ourselves. Earlier, I had thought I would take up common topics a sociologist might identify, like family, career, economics, religion. Yet the more I worried my brain about the most pressing educational duties, I saw that a sociological approach wasn't what was needed.

The four forces I finally chose are "Theyness," "Too Muchness," "Busyness," and "Un-communication." Why such ungainly and unfamiliar terms? The reason is that there aren't any names for these things in common speech and that tells us a good deal about them. When powerful influences in a social network have no accepted names, it means that something is at work to conceal them and hold them away from public contemplation. And that, in turn, means that their functions are deeply repressive.

I'm not so far gone in arrogance as to claim to have discovered these things. In truth, they're being written about with increasing frequency. But the discourses which take them up are spread out over such a variety of disciplines and technical terminologies we're just beginning to recognize what's actually in play and to devise strategies for coping with it.

Education has a major responsibility in countering and transforming each of these four patterns of thought, but it's a responsibility that right now is being undermined by the structures the educational institutions have adopted. The degree salesmen, rather than being critics of the four, have become their agents. Actually, "agent" isn't quite strong enough a word. What they have really become is their "creatures."

I'll spend a letter on each of them, and when I've got through the four, I hope I will have topped off the argument that the universities need to re-think their mission and that the current management will try to subvert the effort rather than assist it. I'll begin with "Theyness."

It's a term that figures pivotally in the thought of the philosopher Martin Heidegger, so I need to mention at the start that he has influenced my thinking about it. But I'll deal with him in the same way I've approached other thinkers, keeping in mind that my purpose isn't to analyze or evalu-ate anybody's philosophy but rather to point out some truths about higher education and the direction it has taken lately. So, having acknowledged Heidegger, I'll hold him in the background and not wade deeply in the swamps pumped up by his idiosyncratic language.

"Theyness" in its ground meaning is pretty simple. It designates a concen-tration on what some generally indistinct body of people are saying, or thinking, or doing, or wanting. Everyone lives with such groups in the back of his mind. Everyone is influenced by them. Everyone fears them to a greater or lesser extent. They work on us in more ways than we recognize, or can recognize. Yet, the most interesting thing about them is that we don't usually know who they are.

I'm not going to suggest that any of us can ever get rid of the "theys" in our lives. It would take superhuman will, and even if we could do it, we couldn't imagine what the results might be. There's at least a good chance they would be monstrous. I've never been one to see freedom as perfect independence from the effects of other people. We are social beings, after all, and any education worth the name has to deal with us as social beings.

We can, however, achieve a partial and healthy emancipation by taking thought about who our "theys" actually are and setting them in an order of importance, and also by negating the pitiful effects some of them have on us by creating new ones that hold us to a higher standard.

The first "they" we all have to confront, and the one that probably does the most damage, is general public opinion: what we imagine our society thinks about success, popularity, appearance, and the damnable quality rotting the brains of the baby-boomers called "coolness." This is the they the advertisers rely on most securely. I saw a commercial just last night showing a guy sitting in the waiting room of a car wash while a powerful, gleaming SUV came down the line. His face was a mixture of longing and shame, which shifted completely in the latter direction when the loud speaker announced that a car was ready at the exit, and he was forced to walk out and get into his old-style station wagon. This was humiliation!

We tend to think that such appeals are so blatant, and so cheap, that no one could pay them any mind. Yet somebody decided to spend a lot of money to make that commercial, and I don't think it was done mindlessly. It was done out of the knowledge that many Americans believe they're being rated by the kind of car they drive. And they care about the rating. That's pretty much where they stop. Few go on to ask: what kind of person would rate another person by his car? Or: what does it say about me that I should care one second about the opinions of such people? We want to be admired, and however shallow the markings that draw admiration, we're eager for them.

As I say, this is inevitable, and not all bad. There is such a thing as taste in material goods, and there's nothing terribly wrong with wanting to be thought a person of good taste. If I were going to a formal gathering I'd feel better in a suit from Brooks Brothers than I would in one I got at J.C. Penny's. The question is not how to banish desires of this kind but how much weight to give them. What will we do to achieve them? What will we give up in order to have them? These are the questions for education, and they can be confronted only through a curriculum deep enough to raise them.

If a student were asked to read, say, *Madam Bovary* and *Great Expectations* and then to discuss the meanings of both novels with a group of curious people, it would be hard to miss the message that we often get ourselves into trouble by wanting too much to be fashionable and sophisticated. And the message would be reinforced by images that stick to the brain: Joe's manner in London when he discovers that Pip is ashamed of him, Emma's contorted face after she has eaten the poison. These are the fruits of un-worthy fashion, and in good teaching they are linked, at least by implica-tion, to similar fashions that pervade our own atmosphere. Many profes-sors think lessons of this kind are too simple to hold their notice, but that's because they forget, or don't care about, whom they are teaching. A public that will buy a car because it wants to feel proud at a car wash needs to be taught some pretty simple stuff.

I read an article yesterday about a real estate development south of Los Angeles called "Oceanfront" where the average price of a house is five mil-lion dollars. There are to be seventy-nine of these behemoths, which run to about seven thousand square feet each, and all of them are pre-fabricated. You might think that if someone were going to shell out five million bucks for a house he would want something distinctive, but that's precisely what the buyers at Oceanfront don't want. One of them was quoted as saying that his house was full of features he liked but would never have thought of himself: "We didn't have to use our imagination and kill ourselves trying to figure out how to do it." No, somebody else did it for him in accordance with what "they" say a successful man's house ought to be.

You might write this off as harmless vulgarity, but I think it goes deeper than that. It sets a measure of what "success" means in modern America and thereby creates goals for young people. A generation of youth who believe that the big thing in life is to live in a garish five million dollar house won't give much attention to wisdom, justice, and moderation, nor will they resist the temptation to rip each other's guts out as they ascend to that standard of imperial ecstasy.

What's the university doing about low-minded aspiration? It's scarcely challenging it. Most university promotion paints higher education as an avenue to this brand of success rather than as a locale for examining it. The reason is not hard to find. The interior "theys" of the university don't prescribe modes of being that offer any clear advance over meretricious consumption. In fact, they present little more than slightly complicated versions of it.

The prevailing "theys" of the university comprise what are called the academic professions. The first truth we need to face about these groups is that their inclination towards service has withered almost to the point of non-existence, whereas their function as guilds protecting the privileges of the members is paramount. What service, for example, do the English professors of America see themselves as rendering to the people of America? Are they committed to spreading the joys of literature through the general population? Are they willing to make sacrifices to insure a mature literacy is widespread? I'll admit there may be remnants of these motives among them, and I want never to fail to honor that small portion of professors who give themselves to their students. But the structures of reward in the profession testify that service is valued least among all the functions guild members perform. The lowest, meanest, most-degrading thing one has to do, from the perspective of a typical English department, is to teach semi-literate students the fundamentals of reading and writing. That's not their job, the professors say. That should have been done in high school. They don't pause to consider that even weak students can be helped to genuine literary appreciation by teachers willing to expend effort. Their effort, by contrast, is spent running away, seeking to spend their days in ever more esoteric pursuits, among students who themselves aspire to the privileges of the guild. As they do, the conversation among them becomes little more than high-fallutin gossip.

I shouldn't single out the English professors. They behave in the same way as their colleagues in the other professions. For most professors, regardless of department, the significant "they" is composed of the voices in their profession, and there is small inclination among them to exchange a substantial word with anyone outside. Why should there be? The "they" of the profession hand out the real rewards: hand out tenure, hand out professorships, hand out grants, hand out university press book contracts. These are the things that count from within. Yet, from the perspective of anyone outside, there's no reason to regard them as finer, or higher, than a fat, ugly house.

I said I was going to stay away from explicit notice of Heidegger. But, I'm at a point now where I need to introduce a concept that's identified with him so strongly it would be dishonest not to give him credit for it. It's widely acknowledged that a fundamental weakness of modern technological society is the sort of fragmentation detailed above, where specialized groups care only for what's going on in their own bailiwick. The main reason for this is that, though many recognize the social futility of what their group does, they think the current system will hold together long enough to get them to their pensions (There's scarcely any rapture more fulgent than the face of a professor reviewing his TIAA-CREF account). We are in the grip of a temporal shallowness where neither responsibility to the past nor care for the future means anything. The reigning practical wisdom says, take care of yourself and yours as long as you're alive, and forget the rest.

Heidegger says this is an inauthentic way to live, and regardless of whatever else that tricky adjective means, it means this: an empty, sick feeling that life is actually of not much account. The cure—which is easier prescribed than taken—is what he called an ecstatic fusion of the past, present, and the future, a fusion that will allow one to believe that though his earthly life is limited by biology, his meaningful life is part of a historical linkage that can't be broken. This is a topic that would require volumes to spell out adequately. I'm bringing it in here to introduce the idea that we needn't be limited to the "theys" that try to box us into a fragment of life. We can put together our own "they" who sustain us in our hope that we'll come to an end that means more than a pension.

Throughout these letters I've alluded to people I admire, and I don't suppose I've mentioned anyone more frequently than Jane Austen. The reason is, she's always in my mind. Not a day goes by when I don't think of her or some of her characters. She is a member of a "they" who are far more vital for me than any current set of professionals because she has more to offer. I would rather have her approval than to win the Bancroft Prize. That doesn't mean I worship her or think she's right in every instance. But I do want to listen to her carefully, and I would think a long time before I did something she would disapprove. She along with perhaps a dozen more make up a "they" for me that work more powerfully than any contemporary group does.

Every student needs a group, a "they," who function in this way. An "education" that is not helping him or her construct one is a paltry thing. It's not sustaining. It offers no courage. It can't function as a support in times of horror. It severs one from history. It's no more than a path to an ugly, empty house.

Heidegger—to bring him in again—says we're in a time when we cannot find vital, ecstatic connections to the past and future. We're in a time that is inevitably inauthentic. I can't be sure about that. But I do know that if we want to get beyond the shallowness that threatens to sweep us away, we need "theys" who stiffen our resolve, make us resolute, give us courage, rather than the common "theys" whose main purpose is to forbid the courage that makes any transcendence possible.

"Theyness," though powerful, is not alone. Next time I'll try to say something about one of its cousins, "Too-muchness."

I'm not sure exactly when we stepped over the line from having too little to having too much. It happened so recently that, despite increasing notice, we haven't seriously begun to think about the problems of crossing over. This letter is little more than a plea that we begin to ask ourselves how it has influenced education.

*T*HE ARGUMENT THAT we're being swamped by too much of everything is hardly original. Scarcely a week passes without my seeing an article or column bemoaning the fragmentation of life caused by over-stimulation. Lately, there's been significant commentary about the inability of Americans to get enough sleep. They have so many things to do they keep chopping the night away.

It's interesting, though, that among all this wave of worry little is said about the impact of "too-muchness" on education. To the degree it's mentioned at all, it's seen as a blessing. We appear hellbent on getting every third-grader plugged into the internet. Presumably, little kids can do their "research" papers more competently when they go surfing through cyberspace. There's no time to stop and ask what vision of education is presented by the concept of a small child sorting through measureless compilations of data.

Some say we live in a millennial, or apocalyptic, time in which the changes rushing upon us are so dramatic our modes of thought can't assimilate them. All we can do is sit back and watch them happen. That was the message of a provocative book published in 1998, by Mitchell Stephens, titled *The Rise of the Image, the Fall of the Word.* Electronic communication has changed everything, said Stephens, and the new world that's coming won't have time for the painstaking, word by word patience that once was the essence of education. Information will be conveyed through images, and not just still pictures, but images flashed on screens at the rate of ten or twelve a second. The kind of knowledge, and the kind of thinking, that will result will be different from bookish learning. It won't be as deep, but it will be broader, and in a globally organized world, according to Stephens, that won't necessarily be a bad thing. People will have a flashing familiarity with a vast range of information, but they won't ponder long over any of it, nor will they be able to articulate their feelings about it. It will be a world of induced instinct, where emotion and action will be driven by images zipping by so fast we scarcely know we've taken them in.

Stephens makes about as good a case for this world as can be made, and some of his points are hard to refute. He knows how television and the internet work, and he has a pretty good grasp of what will be happening to them in the immediate future. Their power, which already seems immense, will multiply at rates we've scarcely imagined. They will sweep away everything that conflicts with their requirements, and there's really not very much anyone can do about it. Even if you can't make yourself like the world that's on the way, you may as well face the truth that it's irresistible.

He may be right, but I don't warm up to arguments of inevitability. They deny human freedom, which, though it has always presented a philosophical dilemma, remains a human need. One thing seems quite clear: a social environment shaped and driven by mass, electronic communications, cycling our attention among a dozen topics a second, cannot sustain the ideal of individual freedom that has been a prime goal of liberal education. A mind that is responding every second is not initiating anything. It has no time for the kind of self-scrutiny that allows fresh ideas to emerge. If we want to hold on to the possibility of personal decision-making, we'll have to take thought about how to do it in a world increasingly marked by flooding of every sort.

At the moment, colleges and universities aren't giving the problem much attention. To the extent the subject comes up, thinking about it takes on a bandwagon aspect. How can we use these new devices to sell more degrees?

is the prime question. What effect the devices are having on education counts for virtually nothing among university managers or faculty members. I have a friend who tried for years to raise the issue with the colleagues in his teaching unit. He was persistently brushed off as a Luddite and, finally, became so frustrated he quit his job and moved to another institution.

At Christmas sometimes you'll notice how the little kids get so many presents they can't concentrate on any one of them. Other presents are always beckoning. After a while frustration causes them to break down in tears. That's getting to be the condition of the human race. We're trying to live our whole lives as though it were Christmas morning every day. It's true with respect to material things, but I think it's even more true with respect to intellectual and artistic stimulation. David Denby, the film critic for the *New Yorker,* said not long ago that living in North America in the 1990s was like being buried alive in cultural sludge.

The effect of this landslide on the college curriculum has been disastrous, but it has opened vast new areas of huckstering for the degree salesmen. Every imaginable speculation becomes an avenue for selling degrees. And since people like to speculate about their grievances more than about anything else, the growth sector in many universities has depended on studies in self-expression. If a person can be awarded a degree by relating the ways other people have mistreated him, or others in his category, and by splashing the account with a few half-digested psychological theories, all educational boundaries are removed and the only limits the degree salesmen have to confront are those imposed by the economic plenitude of their society.

What's wrong with this? one might ask. So what if liberal studies are shifted in the direction of therapy? If people are willing to pay for it, and if society is willing to acknowledge it, what's the harm in having college become simply a process either of telling one's own story or of finding a theory that seems to fit one's own story?

The harm, of course, comes from the damage done to politics—taking the political in its broadest sense as the means for adjudicating common concerns. When everyone knows only his own story, or his own theory, then understanding is only of the self and not of the other. Under those circumstances political discourse is futile. People who comprehend nothing of what the other has known or experienced find it exceedingly hard to talk to one another. When conflicts arise, as they inevitably do in social life, the common practice is to retreat into one's own small circle and glare balefully at everyone else.

I may seem to be going back on myself. Didn't I say that the cascade of cultural stimulus was scattering people's notice everywhere so they couldn't pay attention to any one thing? How can I now complain of people who fail to know things in common? This is where we see the malign genius of too-muchness: it both broadens and narrows. It spreads our mundane attention, which never goes deep enough to matter, everywhere at once, so that we have trouble concentrating. Yet, when we do make the effort to focus, it presents us with so many disparate subjects, we are likely to pick one that puts us in a circumscribed group. Nowhere in the current flood is there encouragement to give lasting thought to issues affecting everybody, and, as a consequence, society-wide interests slide out of the curriculum.

If I'm in a room full of people who have read Boswell's biography of Johnson, I'm unlikely to agree with all of them. But, we'll be able to talk, and we'll have a chance of resolving our differences in a way that's bearable for us all, though some would doubtless find the resolution less pleasing than others. If, on the other hand, I'm in a room of people who have read nothing in common and have had few common experiences, the talk will either remain sterile or descend to heated jabber. Either way, nothing will be resolved, and other, less manageable, means for dealing with differences will eventually arise.

I haven't said much, directly, about friendship in these letters, but I hope I've implied its importance. Without friendship there can be no education worth the name. What role might education possibly play within a populace whose interactions are fleeting and trivial? None that I can see. Education is a process of staying with an idea until you've plumbed its depths, and that doesn't happen through chance encounters. It happens when people give enough of themselves to one another to sort out the implications of something, and that occurs most frequently in friendship, and particularly in friendship where knowledge of substantial matters is involved. Living as we do today, jumping incessantly from one subject to another because so much is calling for our attention, we flush away the possibility of friendship.

Popular culture indicates the truth of our condition by offering fantasies of what we are missing in reality. It's no accident that series like *Friends* and *Seinfeld* have been popular recently. It's no accident that almost every situation comedy shows us a group of friends who spend a great deal of time together, and talk about everything under the sun. These shows make us aware of the absences we feel. Few people actually have the kind of acquaintances who inhabit these programs. I don't think it's an exaggeration to say that most people in modern America don't have a single person with whom they can explore the full implications of their experiences. "Therapy" flourishes because people now have to pay for a semblance of the kind of interaction that should flow naturally from good education.

Gradually, against my will, I've been driven to believe in the existence of an unconscious social force which has no name but which functions as if it had been designed to destroy the possibility of educated minds. It's the Leviathan of our age, but unlike Hobbes's famous conception it is not "the matter, form, and power of a commonwealth" but rather a more nebulous thing, and more powerful for that reason, an uncontrolled social nervousness which operates to convince people that they have no right either to relax or reflect. And the prime weapon of this force is what I've called "too-muchness." I emphasize that I don't view this as any kind of conscious conspiracy. No group of corporate executives meets anywhere to keep it going. Hollywood can't make a movie in which an enterprising young lawyer will find a way to break it up. Yet numerous functionaries throughout society behave as if they were in its employ, and for practical purposes, they might as well be.

Inside the university, the degree salesmen serve it by questing endlessly for something else, something new, something fashionable to put on the block. Old-fashioned literacy has no cachet so old-fashioned literacy is seldom emphasized in the swelling streams of promotional literature university management pumps into the public arena. There can never be enough. There always has to be a new something that will give people a leg-up in the accelerating mania to do more, have more, see more, and control more. This is a game with no winners and increasing casualties. It's the kind of game the university ideally would stand apart from, and criticize, in the interest of social health. But now, the universities are in it up to their eyes.

Given that they are, I foresee no quick or easy reform. The more than three thousand institutions of higher education in America, and particularly the great middling mass which is the object of my attention in these letters, form an interlocking system of finance and vested interest that would be hard put to change its ways even if a significant percentage of its participants became convinced of the need to do it. Systems this entrenched change only when they are bludgeoned into change. Right now it's hard to find anyone with a big enough club to force them to stop and take notice, much less to turn them around. The people who pay the bills could do it, if they had a vision of education strong enough to force the universities to give it mind. The irony is that it's from the university that its patrons should be receiving their vision.

There is, though, protection against discouragement. First, I need to keep continually in mind a point I made early in the series: the educated mind always takes the long view. Every institution that persists over centuries goes through peaks and valleys. If we happen to be in a valley right now, that's just a part of history. It doesn't excuse us from the attempt to get out. And if the university does sometime in the future offer a finer perspective on life and learning than it does now, the efforts made in the valley will count for as much as the efforts of those enjoying the rewards.

Second, the university is a cracked, fissured, rifty sort of place with lots of crevices, and nooks, and out-of-the-way, forgotten back offices where teachers who may not even be recognized by their deans, and have certainly never met their president, are doing things neither deans nor presidents can imagine. Regardless of unfortunate trends and initiatives, education continues to take place. This is the saving grace of the university and is the reason we should all continue to support it, even as we gag over some of things presidents do and say.

Finally, to return to the theme of this letter, there's too-muchness itself which really is too much. More and more people are seeing it. More and more people are trying to find ways to rebel. More and more are asking whether so-called learning that keeps it going is genuinely learning at all. I have no sense of how soon they might coalesce and bring their force to bear on the university, but if notices in popular entertainment and the media are an indication, they are growing faster than the people in charge recognize. Those who love the university need to seek allies among them.

This means, for me, that I'm obliged to push on and write my next letter, where I'll take up a topic allied with the one I've discussed today. "Busyness" has many overlaps with "too-muchness," but it has some special features of its own.

I've persisted in designating the quality I'm addressing here as "busy-ness" (with a hyphen) even though dictionaries have an entry for "busyness." The real word, primarily, conveys a sense of being continuously engaged in activity, whereas my coinage is trying to get at something else, something more psychological than economic.

WHEN I WAS a child I had it in mind to grow up to find a group of companions I could count on for help, company, and conversation. I didn't know precisely how this would occur. It just seemed as though it was the normal thing and, consequently, would come to pass in the ordinary processes of living. Now that I've passed through a goodly portion of my life I hold myself as having been blessed by fine friends, but except for brief periods, I haven't been able to depend on their presence. I knew I could call on them in times of unusual trouble, but for regular purposes, day by day, they aren't around. I don't think my experience in this respect is much different from anyone else's.

The gulf separating me from friends is the same chasm that divides most of us from many of the best fruits of life. I call it "busy-ness."

When I first began to mix in adult organizations, I discovered a phenomenon which has become ever more acute since I first noticed it: the habit of taking an hour to do a ten-minute task. It's particularly prevalent among people who work in offices and among those who spend their lives sending batches of paper to one another. Once you become aware of it, speculation about its causes inevitably follows.

I 'm not talking here about lingering lovingly over a task, savoring its details, musing about its connections, bathing in its aesthetic elements, playing games with its components. These are all essentials of educational activity and deserve encouragement. But I don't think they're what's going on in commonplace busy-ness. Its etiology is more complex and considerably less noble.

In the previous letter I mentioned an unconscious force that might as well be a deliberate conspiracy to control us, because that's how it behaves. At the center of its influence is a nervous worry that we're not doing enough and that other people view us as not doing enough. Where the "enough" comes from is hard to say. Keeping it vague and fuzzy is a requirement of its potency. Its effect, though, is fairly clear and divides into two distinct streams: how we relate to ourselves and how we relate to other people.

I don't mean to imply that when people are jittering about, wearing out their hours on trifling tasks, that they're being either lazy or consciously deceptive. They've convinced themselves that it takes, for example, an hour to write a two-paragraph memorandum and that writing it is the most important thing they could be doing. When people convince themselves of something that's not true, it's generally because they're trying to cover up something else. In this instance, the truth to be concealed is that modern, bureaucratic, technologically-driven humans have only a tenuous grasp on the core of living, the something in life that gives it meaning. People aren't eager to know that about themselves, and the prime way of not knowing is keeping busy. Their vacuity, though serious, and getting more severe as we move towards a life made tolerable only by the ingestion of prescribed chemicals, shouldn't be exaggerated. Contact with the core hasn't been totally severed. Most people retain a vestigial knowledge that something is wrong, that the things that actually matter most to them are not the things on which they're spending the greater part of their lives. That's troubling. But, again, when we're troubled we can partially forget about it by telling ourselves we'll deal with it later. At the moment, there's some other business demanding our attention. For many, that moment ends only in death.

Habits persisted in take on the semblance of fact. It becomes a fact that we have to spend sixty hours a week on tasks that could just as well be done in ten. Furthermore, we lose the ability to ask why we're doing them in the first place. The first lasting demonstration of this organizational vacancy occurred for me when I was a young management intern working for the General Services Administration in Washington, at the headquarters for Region Three, housed in a large building two blocks south of the Mall. I noticed that every incoming phone call had to be recorded on a particular form, which was then placed in an outgoing basket whose contents were collected at the end of the day. I was told that we mustn't miss a single call; it was very important to have the record complete.

One day, I asked my supervisor how the forms were used. He looked puzzled for a moment, then suggested that I find out and write a report on it. Interns, you know, have to be given something to do. I checked with the guy who picked up the forms at the end of the day. He told me he bound them into bundles and took them to an office on the ground floor. I went to the office. There I was told they were kept in a storeroom for six months. What then? At the end of the half-year they were shipped to an office in the basement. I went to the basement, where I found large cartons of the forms, each neatly labeled with its time period. I asked the guy there what he did with them. He kept them for two years. And then? He took them to garbage disposal. At each storage place I asked whether anyone ever consulted the forms. In both places, the workers had been at it more than ten years, and over that period no one had asked to see a single one of them.

I wrote my report and gave it to my supervisor. He commented, "It doesn't seem to be doing much good, does it?" I agreed. And then: "Well it would be a hassle to change it, though." As far as I know, that was the end of it. Since then that process has figured for me as the objective correlative of much administrative work in large organizations. I guess we could say it was harmless. It gave people something to do. In truth, they were proud of doing it well, and it seemed to me it was being done exactly in accordance with regulations. Some might say this is the destiny of humanity: to do work of that kind in return for security, while a small technological elite controls the mechanisms which actually supply the necessities of existence. I suppose this could be seen as a pretty good deal compared with the horrors of the past. But, if it's the deal we opt for then education as it has been conceived is obsolescent.

I've tried to avoid philosophical issues in these letters, but occasionally I find myself pushed up against a fundamental question I can't sidestep. In this case, it's whether humans need anything other than biological security and routine acknowledgement from their fellows. Do we, because of fate, or our nature, or the dictate of God, require anything besides being embedded in a self-sufficient hive? Up till this century the question has been speculative, dealt with mainly in utopian novels such as *Looking Backward* or *Brave New World.* We didn't have the technological know-how to make a hive function, and so, in the effort of some to achieve moderate comfort, we dove into politics, religion, mysticism, and various cosmologies. Out of them came the curious notion that human life should have meaning. Now, however, we're on the verge of something quite big: the possibility that we can construct a human hive where every person will have his little cell and the means to sustain his biological existence for nearly a century. Will this be a heaven, or a hell?

I've answered for myself many times over in these letters. I even answered in the first paragraphs of this one. But I can't expect my opinion to be taken automatically as gospel, and I have to admit that from the perspective of hive-man an educated person may simply be maladjusted. The question of the right way, at least from an educated stance, is deeply personal and has be answered through processes that are to some extent mysterious. I mentioned this problem in my letter about Charles Taylor, and here it is popping up again. And it will always be present whenever we give thought to the goals of our time and effort.

The lesson of busy-ness is that we shouldn't be thinking about things like that. We should get on to the next task our social environment has set before us, and after we complete that one, turn to the next. This is the practical way. Since it is, all prestige—again from the perspective of busy-ness— derives from demonstrating faithfulness to the process. If you want to be a big deal in hive-world your life has to be a matter of schedules. Your calendar has to be packed. You have to consult it every time you ask yourself whether you can take ten minutes out for a cup of coffee, or whether you can go watch your little kid play in a baseball game. And, if you can do the latter often your importance declines to pathos. The ultimate is to be so "professional" that nothing outside the profession can be given a moment's attention. If, in fact, you don't have enough professional stuff to pack every waking minute, you have to fake it. You have to fill up the hour with ten minutes work, and most of all, you have to keep secret from yourself that that's what you're doing.

Educated persons try to keep no secrets from themselves. That's why they're always poorly adjusted.

My greatest surprise, when I began to work in colleges, was to find that few professors have an educational ideal for themselves. They are content to be shaped by their professions, and most are hostile to the idea that education might be something other than professional immersion. This is the reason, by the way, that introductory courses, the famous 101s, tend to be dysfunctional. They are taught as though the students were neophyte sociologists, or psychologists, or economists, et cetera. There's little sense that students should be viewed as men and women with the potential to be well-read. How might they be seen that way, when the professors themselves have no vision of a well-educated person? David Hume used to be noted for having said, "Be a philosopher, yes, but be first a man." But I suppose, now, that's known only to the denizens of philosophy departments, and probably only to those who have chosen the Anglo-American branch, rather than the continental.

The most laughable aspect of academic busy-ness is the argument that it was once possible to survey all knowledge—perhaps three or four hundred years ago—but that now, the evolution of knowledge itself has banished that prospect and has decreed that one devote himself to ever smaller ranges of investigation. How knowledge has anthropomorphized itself to the point that it has a will and can make us do stuff is not usually explained. It's a silly argument from both ends. It has never been possible to know everything, and, consequently the particular things one decides to know have always been a matter of choosing. What varies over history are the mechanisms and reasons for choice. It's true, of course, that in applied sciences, the amount of knowledge required to carry out specific tasks has expanded so that the number of those tasks one person might reasonably attempt has been reduced. But this is a factor that bears on training, not on education. If Heraclitus were miraculously to be resurrected and taught a modern language, he would be more able to engage in educated conversation about the problems of the contemporary world than the average college professor can. The two and half millennia of produced "knowledge" rolled out between his time and ours would be as nothing compared to his ability to think about the one and the many, appearance and reality, and how those philosophic puzzles pertain to modern goals and aspirations. The reason we've been led to believe that we must have narrow minds has nothing to do with the volume of knowledge, and everything to do with the program of modernity. Narrow minds are a requirement of the hive; it can't function as it's supposed to if the functionaries see anything other than the path directly in front of them.

Finally, for education, there are two key questions:

> Do we wish to be functionaries, or something else?
> If something else, what?

We should answer with the understanding that if we say yes to being functionaries, then education has served its purpose, and is over. It can be put on the shelf with other discarded historical practices like human sacrifice, slavery, and the eradication of smallpox. Functionaries have no need of education; they simply have to be trained.

I recognize, of course, that I'm over-simplifying. I said near the beginning of the series that education and training are hard to separate and that they appear to have permanent areas of overlap. If the overlap is, indeed, inevitable, then functionalism can't be a workable solution. That won't keep people from trying for it, though. The more they try, the more the regimen of busy-ness will be intensified, and the more the pathologies that arise from it will permeate social life.

You see what I've done. I've worked my way round to the proposition that education can't accommodate busy-ness. It's the purpose of the latter to see education set aside. We know the maxims about a house divided, and in this instance its truth is supported by evidence that busy-ness will be unrelenting in its efforts to undermine the conversations on which education depends.

I may seem to have strayed from my topic, which is how education can resist the degree salesmen and find a secure home in the university. But I don't think, in actuality, I have. Almost every activity in the university is subject to the assaults of busy-ness, and to the degree they're successful, education's foothold becomes more slippery. I've spoken before about the packaging of learning, so it can be more easily advertized and peddled. The process always requires formularization. Go into any classroom, in any university, sit for ten minutes, and you can see how much busy-ness has taken over. If the class is proceeding methodically, if it's on a strict schedule, if the professor is having conversations neither with the students nor with himself, if the students show a lazy confidence they can get what's necessary from the class by reviewing the syllabus, if, as a consequence, they are laid back, waiting for the bell, if the hour is being given to exactly what was intended before the hour began, if the lesson plan is sacrosanct, then education is absent, and busy-ness is in control. Everyone will go away feeling, temporarily, that he has done what he was supposed to do and proceed to the next task on the schedule, where the same feeling will ensue. If there's any sensation that perfectly bespeaks the death of education, that's it.

So, if not the busy-ness of functionalism, what? If I've made any sense, I've shown that such a question defies a comprehensive answer. But next time, as I end this section with thoughts about the sabotage of communication, maybe I can sketch the outline of a response.

In this series I wasn't able, as much as I intended, to relate the deficiencies of education to the fundamental ills of modern society. To do it adequately would have required a scope beyond the nature of this enterprise. But here near the end I did take a step in that direction which, perhaps, will suggest how other steps might be taken.

W*HEN I BROUGHT* Heraclitus into the previous letter I hadn't yet considered how nicely his style would lead into this one. I need the model of someone who can state a case concisely because the topic of un-communication could metastasize to monstrous length. It touches on everything I've mentioned earlier, and more besides.

In the 91st fragment of his existing writings, Heraclitus says (in the translation by Brooks Haxton):

> Since mindfulness, of all things,
> is the ground of being,
> to speak one's true mind,
> and to keep things known
> in common, serves all being,
> just as laws made clear
> uphold the city,
> yet with greater strength.
> Of all pronouncements of the law
> the one source is the Word
> whereby we choose what helps
> true mindfulness prevail.

"Mindfulness" as used here is nearly the same thing I've been calling education. Certainly, everything Heraclitus says about it is true of education. We have no foundation for individual being unless we educate ourselves. And unless we educate ourselves through things known in common, we lose the ability to converse with either companions or fellow citizens and, thereby, undermine the possibility of a livable commonwealth.

The "Word" gives us the power to choose intellectual habits and the modes of life that lead to mindfulness, or education, and, consequently, keeping it undiluted and unslathered by mental disorder is the duty of all educated persons. "Word" in this sense means, of course, the honorable use of language, the use of language in the service of truth, the use of language to make clear what is being said, the use of language to dig out messages hidden below the level of immediate consciousness.

The language of common practice isn't up to those standards, and the university as it's currently functioning does little to drag it out of the prevailing commercial, political, and psychosocial muck. Truth is, many parts of the university work harder to teach the arts of deception than to stand up for clarity.

The pitiful condition of public language has been bewailed so loudly it may seem useless to add my voice to the chorus. Nearly everyone who examines social discourse seems to conclude that most people are either too lazy-minded to attend to the meaning of words, or too focused on their own advantage to care about using them cleanly. Critics speak as though these stupidities and corruptions define the human condition. But that's not the case. Since there are some people who manage to deal with language honestly, it stands to reason that their number could be increased. How much no one can say. Yet, in education we should continuously remind ourselves that we're dealing in increments. The issue isn't whether some major percentage of people can't do a thing. Rather, it's how much the small percentage that can do it might be augmented. If fifty percent, or sixty percent, or seventy percent of the human race can never use words respectfully, so what? If the percentage that can were boosted from three to five, it would constitute a revolution. If we could establish just that simple point, it would be worth repeating arguments people may think they've already heard too often.

Universities are commonly said to exaggerate their own importance. Critics point out that higher education lacks the ability to transform society or even to make a notable impact on the general state of education. And if one is speaking of modifying the attitudes of the masses the criticism may be valid. If, though, we're counting only the numbers required for small statistical shifts in mature literacy, the potential of colleges and universities rises dramatically. And, given the difference that would result from adding tiny increments to the ranks of the educated, the universities' unwillingness to engage all their students in the careful use of language becomes a misdeed of major proportion.

Richard Mitchell, the so-called "underground grammarian," has been working against this failure for the past twenty-five years. He began with examples of the nonsense penned by the degree salesmen of his own institution, Glassboro State College in New Jersey. But his writing quickly drew so much interest he felt obliged to expand his scope to the inept language in use throughout higher education. His books are enjoyable, particularly the one on the intellectual habits of professional educators titled *The Graves of Academe*. It's peppered with examples of academic prose which establish beyond doubt that numerous professors and administrators have run off the intellectual track. One of my favorites comes from a task force that was set up at Southwest Texas State University to decide whether academic planning was being done right. The task force was supposed to come with a new model for planning, assuming that the current model wasn't up to snuff. With respect to that task, here's what it said:

> An Academic Planning Model must involve a futures planning
> component. Goals should be set for some time in the future. These
> goals should be translated into shorter-term objectives for which
> the degree of detail and concreteness varies inversely with the lead
> time. There should also be reasonable suspense dates for imple-
> mentation of plans and a definitive methodology for evaluation

and feedback. The interfacing of long-term and short-term planning should result.

We have to remind ourselves, Dalton, that this was written by people with advanced academic degrees who were charged by a university with the job of instructing other people how to plan the work of teaching and learning. And they start out by telling us that plans must have a "futures component." I guess that was necessary so no one would try to plan for the past. Then we go on to "goals" that need to be "translated" into "shorter term objectives," Shorter term than what, nobody says, nor does anybody spell out the difference between a goal and an objective, but I guess picky distinctions like that don't matter. Then we have an inverse variation between concreteness and lead-time and, after that, suspense dates for implementation, which, I guess are somehow different from ordinary dates for starting. My poor little dictionary doesn't even list "suspense" as an adjective, but what does it know? Anyhow, after all this has been done, an interface should result, and as everybody knows an interface is a hell of a good thing.

Stuff like this would be funny were it not that it was cranked out by men and women who are supposed to be helping students learn to read, write, and think. What chance do they have with folks like these as their teachers? Students are being led to believe that tripe of this kind bespeaks elevated thought. Once that notion gets in their heads, they're doomed. A few years down the road and they'll be setting up task forces themselves.

We can sit back and launch these Mitchell-like sorties against the enemy forever, and enjoy ourselves in the process. The trouble is, I don't think they make much difference. The people who write meaningless prose and teach it to their students don't know that's what they're doing. Furthermore, they seldom read anything that could teach them better. If they pick up vague rumors of criticism, they can write them off as mere grumpiness and happily return to the business of selling degrees, a business which floats on a tide of non-communication. Anyone who wants to ease them out of the driver's seat is going to have to dig deeper than the mere pointing out of stupidity.

I've tried in these letters to dig a bit, and I hope I've occasionally scratched through the surface. But I haven't got to the source that causes people to run away from educated discourse. My thoughts have been more symptomatology than diagnosis. I dislike that about myself and yet, at the same time, I see I had to sort through the symptoms before I could reason about what's causing them. My topic today—the unwillingness to communicate and the habit of using words for show rather than meaning—gives me a chance to push my spade in slightly deeper. But, it's just a small excavation. Sifting through the layers of our failure to engage words would require a second series of letters longer than this one.

As I've written, I've also been reading. And because of the support you've given me by listening to these musings—I can't, by the way, emphasize how important listening is; it brings ideas forth as frequently as the person who sticks words on the page—I've been led to readings which attempt to lay out the essential disposition of our culture. That after all is where our schooling practices come from. People teach in line with what they think their fundamental purposes are. That's what the degree salesmen are doing.

More and more in my reading a single message begins to emerge: in modern society our driving ambition is control. We want to control everything: nature, other countries, acquaintances, clients, our own minds, feelings, fate, the cosmos. We want it so much that we're driving ourselves insane. Or, so the voices I've been reading say.

I watch more television than I should, mainly because in the evening my brain gets too bleary to do anything else. I wish I had a stronger mind, but I reflect there are lessons even in vice and puniness. The insight I get from TV is the subtlety advertisers have developed in persuading us to do things we would never think of doing had we not fallen into their hands. That's always been the goal of hucksters, but I doubt that ever before it's been done as skillfully and I'm certain it has never before had the influence it does now. Television has become the leading instructor in language, and it's not teaching anybody to engage in discourse.

Commercials are the best thing on TV. They should be because they're the reason television exists. The programs are simply lures to help get the commercial hooks into us. You'll notice that drug companies are prominent on television now, and their main device is the illusion that everybody has a warm, chatty relationship with a physician. *Ask your doctor if such and such is right for you.* You can bet your dollar that when they say "your doctor" rather than "a doctor" it's no accident. They're creating a world of caring corporations and leisurely physicians into which you can confidently pour your money, a world, by the way, which exists only in flashing images on the screen.

There's nothing inherently evil in persuasion, or in flattery. We all practice them and hope to see some of the latter coming our way. But when they dominate speech to the point that people expect to be oleaginized every time anybody talks to them, then discourse is down the drain, and with it, education. When people lose the ability to speak their minds without being afraid of how they're going to be received, they've transformed themselves from a population of independent minds to a gang of toadies. And, everybody knows the idea of educating a toady is farcical. The language of control is ultimately a language of fear, a language which bespeaks inequality. It is not the language of free people.

History teaches us that in totalitarian countries, everyone watches his words and few dare say what they mean. After a time, most people lose the ability to think of meaning and begin simply to parrot what has been handed down as acceptable. Real communication among the citizens shrinks to furtive whispers. When we begin to observe similar tendencies in a nominally free society, it ought to pique our curiosity. We haven't reached the stage where popping off has been legally squelched, and I guess we can be thankful for that. But it is increasingly relegated to soapbox impotence, whereas talk among the respected members of society becomes ever more formularized. People speak as they're expected to speak. Politicians talk like politicians, lawyers talk like lawyers, bankers might as well be programmed. When is the last time you heard a college president say anything other than what you knew he was going to say before he opened his mouth? This is the language of people who are under control and who are striving to control others. They don't conceive of using words for any purpose other than getting others to do what they want. They are terrified by discourse.

We have no Hitler here. But we do have a system, the uncomprehending, unconscious system I've mentioned before. And it's a system hostile to communication because it's obsessed with control. Such a system can't tolerate education because the primary purpose of education is to enable people intelligently to manage themselves rather than be controlled by others. Richard Mitchell says we have to choose between schools as instruments for prescribed socialization or as incentives to thoughtfulness. They can't be both.

We would do well to get a few leading truths in mind:

> Where control is venerated, communication is twisted.
> Where preset socialization rules, mindfulness is despised.
> Where salesmanship dominates, education languishes.

I have only two letters left, so they have to take the form of winding up. There are many things I might have done here I haven't done, many approaches I might have been expected to take that I haven't attempted, many paths I might have gone down that I haven't been willing even to stick my toe into. Next time, I'll try to explain my reasons for not addressing this topic as might have been anticipated. After that, there'll be space only for some punctuation.

All the time I was sending these letters I was aware they didn't conform to what most people expect of institutional criticism. I hoped that the letters themselves were an adequate explanation of why they didn't. Yet, here at the end, I decided it would be best to deal with the divergence explicitly.

*T*HESE LETTERS HAVEN'T turned out to be what most people would have expected if they had been told beforehand that I intended to write about the problem of education within the university. I had an inkling at the start that they wouldn't run down a beaten track, but when I began I wasn't sure about how they would diverge. Now I see the reason more clearly.

It has taken the writing of the series to teach me, finally, how my concerns differ from those who identify themselves with current university functions. In making this distinction, I'm not eager to set myself apart. It would be better not to have to talk about it. But I have to acknowledge the difference to explain the nature of what I've been doing. It's not an approach that's advantageous. Actually, it's debilitating as far as immediate influence goes. I don't know where it came from, and I've wished at times I could rid myself of it. But, I can't. I feel queasy saying even this in a letter that's not about me but about higher education. I suppose I have to fall back on the plea Thoreau made at the beginning of *Walden*:

> Moreover, I, on my side, require of every writer, first or last, a simple and sincere account of his own life, and not merely what he has heard of other men's lives; some such account as he would send to his kin-

dred from a distant land; for if he has lived sincerely, it must have been in a distant land to me.

To be identified with university life, to view oneself as a university person, means that the university, through whatever evolution it chooses for itself, remains one's principal interest. That membership, that feeling of belonging, that being a part of affairs, that security in university prestige stands above any particular action the university may or may not take. It's an extremely powerful allure, more powerful than most people on the outside can imagine. For many university people it is the essence of existence.

What this means is they're prepared to remain with the university wherever it goes. And if it goes some place they didn't expect, well, it's still the university, and they are still inside. That's what counts. I can't say what percentage of professors, deans, and presidents fall into this category. But my observation tells me that, taking them collectively, it is very high. And when we come to people who choose to write books about university matters, it's higher still. Consequently, the majority of published works that take up teaching and education within the university perceive them as university problems rather than as human problems.

I hope I've made clear by now how my perspective is different. Though I've spent a good deal of time around colleges and universities, I've never been won over to them as ends in themselves, and so, I don't care about them in the way they are commonly appraised. At this point, it might clarify things simply to list the ways in which my caring about universities is less than avid:

I don't care about them as political entities.

I don't care about them as centers of morality (except of the sort that's peculiar to educated discourse).

I don't care about them as career tracks.

I don't care about them as exemplars of any religious tradition.

I don't care much about them as training institutions (training, though important, can be done just as well, and usually better, elsewhere).

Most of all I don't care about them as businesses.

If you take all these forms of caring and match them to the primary concerns and the daily efforts of university employees (of the professional class, of course), you will have encompassed at least nine-tenths of the total energy expended in American universities as they are now constituted. The premise of these letters is that nine-tenths is too much. Education deserves more than the droppings from the table.

Since my concerns are different, it's natural for my methods to be different also. I wouldn't claim that there's even a dollop of social science in anything I've written to you. These letters have been based not on data, as it's commonly conceived, but on observation and experience. It might be said that no single person's experience could be broad enough to justify commentary about the generality of colleges and universities, that only through the data, as the social scientists say, can we discover truth about anything as vast as the American university system. That's not so, and the nature of its falseness tells us something about the withering of education among university people.

The turn to social science as the foundation of social understanding has had a number of bad effects, and perhaps the worst has been the delusion that truth is simply a matter of properly shaped information—put the data into the right configuration and magically the truth emerges. This is a ludicrous belief and, yet, it is widely held. It bypasses the problem of where the shapes come from and proceeds on the largely unexamined assumption that they are inherent in the data themselves. Not only does this magical data/manna contain the truth, it is also possessed of knowledge of how to present itself.

We would do well to remind ourselves, everyday, of something Nietzsche said:

> Having kept a sharp eye on philosophers, and having read between their lines long enough, I now say to myself that the greater part of conscious thinking must be counted among the instinctive functions, and it is so even in the case of philosophical thinking; one has here to learn anew about heredity and "innateness."

If that's true of philosophers, it is bound to be true of other thinkers, and I would argue it's particularly true of social scientists. They are no more free of intellectual impulses than any other category of persons, and so they find ways to persuade the data to support their "instincts." The way we approach the truth is not by sitting around cramming facts into our favorite instinctual packages but rather by bringing our instincts into an open forum and watching how they interact with the instincts of others. This isn't always as comfortable a process as the techniques of social science, but it is the way of education. Also, it happens to be the action that makes us human.

I've tried over the past months to survey the current literature of higher education. Most of it is unappealing because, from my perspective, it both relies unreasonably on social scientific data and it has its priorities backwards. It's concerned, in the main, with the aggrandizement of some portion or aspect of the university and very little with the nature of service the university should be offering. Most accounts of university problems take for granted the virtue of the basic configuration; they just want to tinker a bit with the internal mechanisms.

Even the best of these works appear unable to confront the main issue. Last year, for example, Annette Kolodny published a well-received volume titled *Failing the Future: A Dean Looks At Higher Education in the Twenty-First Century.* The reviewer for the *New York Times* called it "a book of great good will and impeccable good intentions." I don't doubt that's true. Ms. Kolodny sees that higher education is seriously deficient, but she seems to think it can be reformed through budget reallocations within the institutions. The right people, in her view, are not getting the right amount of money. This is a naive perspective. You can shift budgets till kingdom come, and unless a significant portion of the university inhabitants change their attitudes about education it won't make a bit of difference. I know that some say structural changes are what cause changes in belief. But I've been through enough reorganizations to know that however the charts are modified, instrumental beliefs keep pushing education to the periphery. Reform through structural shift is a social scientific dogma in which I have no faith, especially with respect to universities.

Ms. Kolodney is right to say that universities don't spend money wisely. Far too much of it goes to selling, and too little to teaching. When I wrote budgets for the program I headed twenty-five years ago, fifty percent of the income was regularly assigned to faculty salaries. Now, in that same program, I'm pretty sure not even a quarter of the income goes to pay teachers. The same shift has taken place throughout universities all over the nation. One could write volumes describing how university interests have transmogrified, using data from careful analysis of budgets. But when those volumes were in hand, all you would have would be testimony that universities have become different sorts of beasts than they used to be. You still wouldn't know why. Nor could you predict how changing the allocations would modify the nature of the institutions. That's because budgets alone can't tell you about structures of belief. And it's the latter that determine the fate of education in the university. I would take pleasure from seeing faculty members added and assistant directors of admissions dropped from university employee roles, but, within current frames of thought, I couldn't assure anyone that education would benefit thereby.

The reforms generally offered by professors are cleverly constructed to identify education with professorial activity. But read carefully they display more concern for professorial well-being than they do for educational vitality. I've talked to lots of professors who pound the table in favor of smaller classes. But if you ask them how fewer students would modify their teaching, most have little to say. Fewer students means, for them, fewer papers to grade.

The readership addressed by most works on higher education is the popu-lace of higher education. The reader addressed by these letters is you, or anyone who's like you in being an intelligent citizen of the world who cherishes universities more for how they might enrich the world than for how they might enrich themselves. I can't emphasize enough how insular universities are, how perfectly their attention is directed to the goings-on within their confines. Other professions are self-interested, of course, and care more about themselves than they do about anyone else. But they differ from higher education in that they don't have the ability, by themselves, to define the services they deliver or the goals they seek. A physician who regularly killed all his patients would, after a while, begin to be less in de-mand regardless of his professional status. If a lawyer lost every one of his cases, it wouldn't matter how much law he knew. By contrast, universities can continue for decades to fail to teach their students to read and write maturely, to think clearly, or to observe accurately, and few seem to notice. The reason is that universities have managed to identify education with the receipt of degrees, and degrees are things higher education can deliver. It's a sweet deal.

That won't change until universities see that patrons and clients of higher education—persons like yourself—recognize that educationless degrees are a cheat. If they maintain their status as the primary product of univer-sities, if they persist as tokens of nothing other than themselves, degrees will continue to promote corruption. University officials will keep on ped-dling them with small concern for what they represent. The only reason a salesman has for improving or changing a product is a shift in customers' attitudes. As long as the people who buy are gullible and satisfied, trade in shabby goods will thrive.

The degree salesmen don't worry about a shift in attitude because they think they are the creators of it. If they define education as the receipt of degrees, that's what education will be because there's no independent mind outside the university world to conceive of it as anything else. The prevail-ing conceit throughout higher education is the conviction that outside its auspices virtually no one thinks. Consequently, there can be no audience for discussions about education as a process existing in its own right among people generally.

I think this is a mistaken—and arrogant—belief. Universities don't own education any more than English departments own Jane Austen. And since education is not a university possession, the university has no right to shape it as it will. We need to get clear in our minds what is the larger thing here. Yes, the university system is huge, powerful, and influential. But however vast, it is nothing compared to the reach of education, which is a potential bestowed on every human, regardless of schooling.

Human beings don't have to go through universities in order to speak to one another. They don't have to use the jargon of higher education in order to take one another seriously. They don't have to ask the university's permission to be allowed to take up subjects of high import. They don't have to open their mouths to glug down whatever university departments decide to pour in as education. They don't have to beg the university for the right to think.

Humans can come into that space that's generally known as freedom and share their thoughts openly. In the process they can refine their thoughts and make them stronger, and sharper, and more in keeping with sanity and reality. Universities should be promoting these processes rather than trying to control them for the sake of making money from them. I believe there are great numbers of people who understand this, and they are the ones I hope to address in these letters, using you as their proxy. And it's because I'm talking to you, and not to professors or educational administrators, that these discussions have strayed from the common path.

My next letter is the last. I'll see if I can find words to underscore the dysfunction that has tried to pull the university and education apart.

In the final letter, which makes a bow at summary, I try to emphasize that though the education of the future must draw on the best traditions of the past, relying on them is not enough. The coming world demands a new education, but one that incorporates the best that we have known.

I'M NOT READY to finish, but I must. These letters have been, at best, a sketchy introduction to the kind of thinking we have to do if our colleges and universities are going to play a part in keeping education alive. When I say "kind of thinking" I don't mean to imply that my thoughts are adequate or that they should serve as a model for anyone. I mean only that they have circled round the questions that need to be asked.

Those questions aren't being asked with the energy required in the general society, nor are they being asked by the majority of people charged with guiding the middling institutions of higher education in America. I trust I've made clear, throughout, that my focus is on the great mass of schools which enroll at least ninety-five percent of American college students. Most books on higher education differ from my remarks in that they draw their examples from the elite institutions. That may be because their professors are the only ones able to get such writings published. But whatever the reason, as I've said before, if you were to go to the average bookstore and thumb through its collection on higher education you would likely get the impression that students are typically enrolled in institutions like Harvard or Princeton.

I don't know a great deal about Harvard or Princeton. The little I do know tells me they aren't free of problems, educational and otherwise. But these aren't the same problems most colleges face. The graduates of the famous institutions are better educated, in a traditional sense, than are those of the mass. But that's mainly because Harvard and its kin get more eager and better-read students in the first place than the middling places do. It's not hard to energize people who are determined to be educated and who have at least an inkling of what that might mean. The average college, by contrast, has to battle against conventional notions of success even to introduce the possibility of education to the minds of its students. And out in the great stretches of the more than three thousand institutions that remain nameless to most people, there's too little battling taking place.

Perhaps it's an insane idealism to expect all college students to be served by teachers who are trying to bring their minds alive and help them escape from rigid social molds. But if so, I'm guilty of it.

The assumption that only the most prestigious institutions have any reason to put their students in touch with the best that has been thought and said—to use Matthew Arnold's famous formulation—is the doctrine of a perverted democracy which believes that since money is the measure of all things, equality can be served only by training the masses to bait their hooks for big money. It's doubtful that such thinking actually promotes economic leveling, but what we know it does promote is vulgarization of the whole. If a dominant majority of the graduates pouring out of our colleges and universities believe that the main reason they went is to have a cleaner shot at high-paying employment than other young people of their age, then we're in for an ugly social world.

John Henry Newman once said that the mark of an educated mind is the ability to recognize the condition of enough. When a thing has reached the stage of being what it needs to be, there is no reason in trying to exaggerate its capacities. A bedroom of six hundred square feet is no better than a bedroom of two hundred and fifty square feet. A car that will run a hundred and fifty miles an hour is no better, for ordinary purposes, than one that will go ninety. A dinner that costs twenty-five dollars can be just as satisfying, and certainly as nutritional, as one that costs hundreds. These simple lessons our society cannot learn, and the inability to learn them is driving us to distraction.

The cost of unnecessary, and garish, expansion is not just waste—though it, by itself, is serious. Yet, the more devastating price is diversion from finer activities. The expenditure of life required to reside in a million dollar house is, more often than not, ghastly. As one makes his shell, his externals, ever more impressive, the kernel of self is withering away to something pathetic. This is an old, somewhat tired, story and would have no place in a commentary about majoritarian education were it not that we are entering a stage of social development where dreams of million dollar houses and two hundred thousand dollar cars are becoming realizable for those who are willing to devote their existence to them.

When the symbols of extreme monetary success become not just daydreams, as they have been for most people in the past, but, instead, the actual driving force of their lives, then the responsibility of education shifts dramatically. When Matthew Arnold was preaching that students should be taught the best that has been thought and said, the deficiency society needed most to overcome was ignorance. Were he able to walk around among us today I'm pretty sure he would see that though ignorance is still with us and needs to be confronted, the prime foe of education nowadays has become a thoughtless vulgarity that is always seeking to put secondary things before the primary. The degree salesmen, after all, are not ignorant people in the ordinary sense of the term. But they are vulgar. I don't mean to say that they are willfully vulgar or that they lack conventional good manners. But when people charged with helping students reach their educational potential consistently turn them away from education in order to promote secondary activities, vulgarity is the right word for what they're doing.

I've reluctantly come to the conclusion that schooling that might have been educationally adequate in 1950 wouldn't be adequate today. It would be better than what most people are getting, but it would lack the defensive component needed for guarding against the modern rush. In 1950, most people were still afflicted by informational poverty. The teacher's principal task continued to be, as it had been for centuries, finding ways to ensure that students got the information required for intelligent deliberation. By choosing the right study materials and insisting that students digest their main points, the teacher was doing most of what was needed. Now, we are in a new world where information is everywhere. Push a few buttons and you can have, a few inches in front of your face, texts and data that used to require days of digging in libraries. The flood of information is so fierce many feel their minds are being swept away by the current. It's obvious that when the conditions of learning change that radically, the practices of teaching need to make adjustments.

If I were forced to oversimplify, I'd argue that the prime teaching question used to be: "What did this book say?" Now it needs to become: "Okay, now you've read this book, so what?" If you think about those questions a bit you see that the teaching duty moves from explication and examination to conversation. I don't want to overdo the shift. The book still needs to be read and understood. But through searching conversation a teacher can tell whether the student has read the book, and if he hasn't, then measures can be taken to encourage him to read it.

Thoughtful people have known for a long time that unless learning "takes," unless it is integrated into life, it will be little more than decoration. In the past, we operated on a faith that if provocative material were proffered in an atmosphere of intellectual seriousness, then it would take sufficiently to make a contribution to the lives it touched. And, often, it did. That, though, was at a time when, despite occasional bromides to the contrary, we didn't expect more than a small minority to be serious about education. We also expected then that the preliminary attitudes necessary for education, the habits of speaking and listening carefully, would be assured by the domestic upbringing of anyone who aspired to be educated. I don't know how true that ever was, but, certainly, it's true no more. Now, if we can take what we say about ourselves seriously, we expect virtually everyone to have the opportunity for education. Yet, the majority of people are seldom in the presence of educated discourse, and most are never in a situation where they have a genuine chance to practice it themselves. How are they supposed to learn it?

The degree salesmen have no answer. Furthermore, they demonstrate consistently that they never seriously consider the question. In their eagerness to sell degrees and to reduce their own costs to a minimum, they regularly undermine opportunity for educated conversation in institutional life. "Throw information at them electronically," they say. "It's cheaper that way, and besides, they get more of it." But the point is not getting more; the educational issue is learning what to do with what we have.

The degree salesmen are in the grip of the instrumental mania which infects most of the rest of society. This means that virtually all that people do, when they take themselves seriously, is done in the interest of something else. In the state of busy-ness we see around us, action is simply an instrument for producing something else. But what? Nine times out of ten, the thing produced is itself an instrument leading to another, and so on till death. We steadily fail to reach the action that is done for itself alone. And in those cases where we think we've reached it, we call it recreation and trivialize it thereby. We play golf. What a world, where the end reason for the struggle, and the backstabbing, and the undermining, and the outdoing, and countless hours of misery is that old men may play golf! I doubt that people really believe this. But that's the way they talk.

Perhaps the most vexing question we face is what it means to be human. Aristotle argued that only those actions which can clearly be distinguished from animal behavior deserve the designation. As we learn more about the other animals, we become increasingly suspicious of facile claims of human superiority. Yet, Aristotle was right in the sense that if humanity means anything, it must denote something that distinguishes us from other forms of life. One explanation has been that humans seek meaning, whereas, as far as we can tell, the other animals use their intelligence solely to manipulate their environment. If there's validity in the distinction, then the process by which we try to discover, or to make, meaning deserves a name specific to itself. As you know, the best name I've found for it is education.

You might say my whole reason for writing these letters has been to plead that we allow education to be itself and to argue that, as itself, it deserves a central place in the institutions we say are devoted to it.

Aristotle also said that man is the political animal, meaning that humans are destined to live in social units that require deliberation about common purposes. In truth, there's a fairly close correspondence between politics and education, or there would be if our political life were operating as it should. Much of what can be said of one is valid for the other. They both depend on the creation of space between people in which meaning has a chance to manifest itself. I know that may sound, on first hearing, overly metaphysical, but it's a simple concept actually. When we consider the events that give life its majesty they virtually all involve action between people. One person writes and another reads; one person sings and another listens; one person plays and another watches; one person talks and another talks back. When we diminish the quality of what happens in those interactions by transforming it into something formulaic, mechanical, and prosaic, where are we? Who are we? If meaning doesn't find its place in what we do between and amongst ourselves then I can't see that it has real existence. Religious sensibilities might say that it resides between the self and god, but since most religious traditions set the path to god in our treatment of others, the interactive space between one person and another retains its primacy.

What can we say to one another such that the saying flows into the space between us and stands there as a good in itself? That's the question for education. Finding those words is what education is charged with doing. When anything or anyone tries to turn it from that task, and subvert it to other purposes, we are in the presence of educational betrayal.

In a world where betrayal is as common as it is among us, it's hard to know who the betrayers are. It's even hard to escape being one yourself. But, at least we can refuse to give up on action that offers hope of a way around aimlessness. So, here at the end of these letters, let's pledge to one another to use the strength we have to help meaning strengthen itself in the republic, and especially in the universities, which are supposed to be its home, but which are being crippled by the worship of utility. And let's do it not so much by launching projects—although if a good project came along, that would be okay—but by remaining friends, and talking together. There's nothing so fearsome to false utility as friendship, and no other place where meaning can take as firm a hold. When friends sit together and try to make sense of their experiences, the story of what they say can filter out to the world and teach it the promise of education.

I've enjoyed writing to you over these weeks, and the thing that made it best was knowing you were willing to listen, no matter how fumbly my thoughts were. If I could bequeath only one thing to education it would be a population of listeners such as you.